Horses Don't Care About Women's Lib

by

Don Blazer

Joyce Press, Inc.
San Diego, California
1978

ISBN Number: 0-89325-010-4

Library of Congress Catalog Number: 78-53437
Published in the United States by:
Joyce Press, Inc., 7341 Clairemont Mesa Blvd., No. 115
San Diego, California 92111
First Printing

Material in this book has previously appeared in print as columns for Don Blazer's syndicated newspaper column, "Of Course, A Horse."

JOHN WAYNE

Horses have carried me through a very pleasant life, in to many a green pasture. Any thunder, or lightning, or barbed wire in my life has been caused by me - not by any actions of my friend, the horse.

You can learn a lot about horses and people if you read Don Blazer's book. He knows more than a little about both.

Dedication

So many book dedications are sickeningly sentimental. I don't want mine to be that way. I want it to say simply how I feel about two people who made this book possible.

And, so, I'll say it that way.

This book is dedicated with love to my mommy and my daddy.

CHAPTER I

Of Course, A Horse

Dear Mr. President:

The horse just may be able to solve a number of national and international problems for you and alleviate that nagging environmental problem.

Environmentally, the horse is just about perfect.

And since it's "sheik" to save gasoline, the horse could certainly reduce our dependence on Mideast oil.

Whisk away that choking, smoky blanket of smog. The horse is not a polluter, as are man's inventions.

And the U.S. Postal Service might look into Pony Express history for some tips on easing its high-cost, slow-delivery problems.

When you examine the horse's impact on the human environment, you'll find the horse has many all-American characteristics in his favor, and essentially none that detract.

From a public health standpoint, the horse poses no threat to people. No equine disease exists in this country which affects man, and further, the horse is not the natural carrier or source of any disease which can be transmitted to man, according to Dr. James T. O'Connor, president of the American Association of Equine Practitioners (AAEP).

By nature, the horse is friendly, inspiring and harmless. He never molests, attacks or threatens anyone unless forced to do so by man's abuse, says O'Connor.

Inherently, he is a clean animal and is neither a litterbug nor a true polluter.

He leaves no nondegradable litter along the trail or anywhere else. His droppings, says O'Connor, disintegrate rapidly and become the best of soil fertilizer – a side benefit which has been most useful to man for thousands of years.

On the trail, he leaves no continuous tracks and his passing is not conducive to soil erosion.

The horse can negotiate rough and tangled terrain in any kind of weather, vastly reducing the cost of trail construction and maintenance, both necessary for the eroding wheeled vehicles which use our trails.

Of course, the horse doesn't use petroleum products as a source of energy, so he doesn't make us dependent on Mideast oil, as do the bus, train, airplane and automobile.

Let the oil barons raise oil prices. What does the horse care?

And, Mr. President, many a great leader rode a horse to victory.

Think of it! The romance, the appeal, the glory, and half the nation's problems disappearing with the fading sounds of hoofbeats as you ride the campaign trail.

Horses Don't Care About Women's Lib

In the world of horses, there is no Gloria Steinem and no equality.

Male chauvinist that he is, the stallion rules supreme He is always the highest ranking member of the group.

Even among mares and geldings, the selection of which will be the leader and which will follow is made quickly and easily. Once decided, the leadership is jealously guarded.

The pecking order is established by temperament, not size or strength. And it is most often the older and wiser which rules.

Put a number of horses together in a pasture and they soon work out by themselves a society in which every member has a place. Kicking and biting may never occur while the formal hierarchy is being established. Simply the suggestion of strength, such as ears flat back and teeth bared, is all that is required from those which will lead.

And the horses of lower rank do not feel unhappy or oppressed. They experience only momentary frustration. Once they accept their place, they are happy and secure, well aware of just what they may or may not do.

Once established, this equine society is everlasting, at least until a new member is introduced. Immediately he is put in his place, and then he, too, is happy and secure.

Observation of this horse behavior can help the horseman.

Having watched the pecking order being established, the horseman knows the proper paddock arrangement. The horses have already decided for him which ones can be safely stabled together, and which should be in adjacent stalls. The possibility of injury to the horses through fighting is reduced and fences are saved.

Also, if you understand there is no equality among horses, their handling is easier and safer.

The key to handling the stallion is to assert the idea of your supremacy. This is not done by using brute force or severe punishment. It is done through attitude and immediate aggressive action if your leadership should be questioned. Backing away is not tolerated.

The horse follows and obeys strong, confident leadership.

As a French horseman once observed, "Horses, like women, dislike weakness."

The same quiet confidence must be shown when handling mares and geldings. The natural horseman has it, even though he may not label it as such. It is expressed in his manner, his touch, his movement, his thoughtfulness.

It is this natural attitude which makes it possible for some people, even children, to handle almost any horse, even certain stallions. And the lack of it keeps many people from being able to handle any horse.

It is claimed, and I believe it is true, that a swifter, but lower-ranking horse will not outrun a slower, but higher-ranking horse. When they are thundering down the stretch, head and head, eye to eye, the race goes to the winning temperament, not necessarily to the speediest.

Yes, frustration, anxiety and unhappiness abound in the equal world of Gloria Steinem.

But security and peace of mind are the glories of the unequal world of horses.

Eye Of The Beholder

There's just no accounting for some people's taste. Which is why no two people see the same horse in the same way.

"My, what a pretty horse," she says.

"I don't like him," he replies.

"Pretty is as pretty does," another comments.

"This ain't no beauty contest," says the racehorse trainer.

One of the common methods of judging a horse is to examine the horse's conformation and make a determination as to how well that particular horse will perform work.

What kind of work?

Some people want a horse to walk down the trail.

PARTS OF THE HORSE

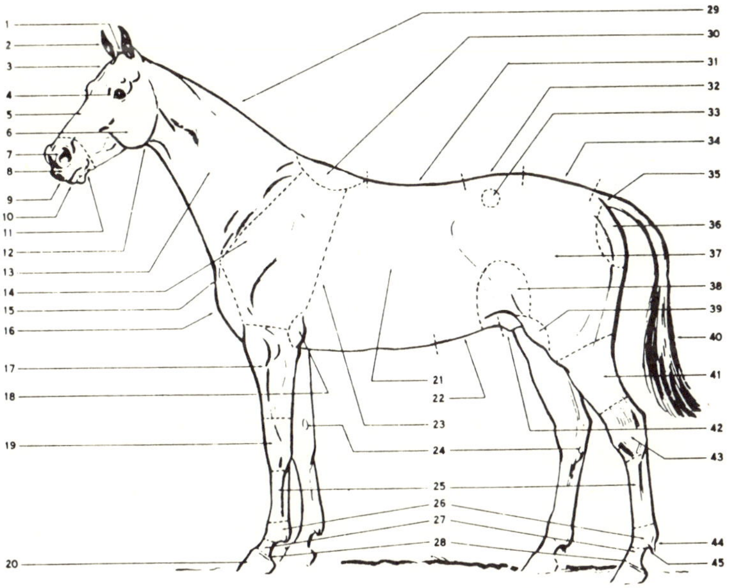

1. POLL
2. EAR
3. FOREHEAD
4. EYE
5. FACE
6. CHEEK
7. NOSTRIL
8. MUZZLE
9. UPPER LIP
10. LOWER LIP
11. CHIN GROOVE
12. THROAT LATCH
13. NECK
14. SHOULDER
15. POINT OF SHOULDER
16. CHEST
17. FOREARM
18. ELBOW
19. KNEE
20. HOOF
21. BARREL
22. ABDOMEN
23. HEART GIRTH
24. CHESTNUT
25. CANNON
26. FETLOCK JOINT
27. PASTERN
28. CORONET
29. CREST
30. WITHERS
31. BACK
32. LOIN
33. POINT OF HIP
34. RUMP OR CROUP
35. DOCK
36. BUTTOCK
37. THIGH
38. FLANK
39. STIFLE
40. TAIL
41. GASKIN OR SECOND THIGH
42. SHEATH
43. HOCK
44. FETLOCK
45. ERGOT

Others want the horse to compete on the show ring rail. Still others want the horse to cut cattle, do a reining pattern, or jump, or pull a wagon.

So, beauty again reverts to the eye of the beholder.

Does the answer lie in the standards established by breed associations?

Not at all. Such standards are artificial, and most often are not in keeping with the way the American horses live and work.

As an example, an American Horse Show Association carded judge told me the Arabian should have a flat croup because it helped keep his hindquarters from sinking into the sands of Egypt. I don't know if his theory is correct — no two Arabian owners have ever told me the same story about the desirability of a flat croup. Yet the flat croup is a breed standard, even though American Arabs seldom, if ever, are worked on sand dunes.

Conformation for the sake of health and soundness might be the best way to judge a horse.

If so, the horse should have an average-sized head, proportionate to the horse in total. The eyes should be large and set well out to the side of the head. The nostril should be fairly large so the horse breathes freely. The ears should be of average size, with a nice little curve in at the ends, and a nice point. The ears should be carried well forward. A broad forehead is desirable, and the jaw should be well-defined, but not overly accentuated. The neck should be fairly long and not heavy in the crest, and the throatlatch should never be thick.

The shoulder should slope at about a 45-degree angle, permitting the horse to raise and lower his head easily, and providing for a long underline and deep heartgirth and, usually, a short, strong back. A short-backed horse carries weight better than a long-backed horse and is usually quicker.

The long underline keeps the front and rear feet far enough apart that the horse does not interfere with himself. It also provides the room necessary for large lungs and a good digestive system.

The hindquarters are the driving unit, or power plant, for the horse. The croup should be long with plenty of muscle over the hips. The muscle at the rear of the hindquarters should extend well down into the gaskin area. When viewed from the side, the hind legs should be squarely under the horse, never out behind him. The hock should be wide and strong, and the point of the hock should not turn in or out.

The pastern should be at a 45-degree angle to match the shoulder, as should the hoof. The pastern absorbs the shock of the horse in motion. Too straight a pastern causes bone and joint problems. Too sloping a pastern causes tendon troubles.

The hoof should be in the shape of a U. Wide at the heel, the hoof should be fairly deep at the rear quarter, and when viewed from the front, should have the same degree of slope on the inside as the outside.

The knees should be fairly large and flat, neither being back or being over when viewed from the side. The fetlock joints should appear strong, but not overly large.

No one can fault my selection of a horse for several reasons. My first two reasons are factually correct, and my final reason is irrefutable.

First, the horse must have the disposition and physical attributes to do the job I want.

Second, hopefully, he'll remain healthy and sound.

Finally, I like him.

A Million Ways To Get Stuck

When it comes to buying a horse, there must be at least a million ways to get stuck with a bad one and about five ways to get a good one.

To get a good horse, you have to use a little common sense. Emotion is the villain.

It's natural to be excited by the thrill of owning a new horse. But, whoa, hold it. Shorten the reins!

I know the horse is beautiful and the story that goes with it is reasonable and the horse may be sold tomorrow, but accept some hard-to-take advice. Buyer, beware!

Before you start looking for a horse, decide what it is you want and write down your requirements. Your list should include breed, size, age, amount of training, color, sex and price. You're the only one that knows exactly what you want and you're the one who must be satisfied.

Now don't let emotion cloud your view. The horse you buy should meet your requirements or you'll be unhappy later.

If you have decided you want a color breed, then color is important. But, remember, color doesn't make a horse perform, so always examine the horse's way of going, his conformation and his disposition.

Think about your physical relationship with the horse. Is he too big, or too small? As a team, do you look well together? And in three years, after you've invested your money, time and effort, how will the horse look?

And, don't forget, a good horse doesn't cost a dime more to keep than a bad horse. Registered horses eat the same food, have the same vet bills, wear the same-priced shoes, but their value is almost always greater.

Bargain horses usually aren't bargains, so beware of sad stories, auctions and the fast deal.

Well-known horse trainers are most often the best people to see. They have a reputation to protect and seldom, if ever, will they let you get stuck with a bad horse. A bad horse can hurt a trainer's reputation in a hurry.

So now that you know what you want and you have a good place to start looking, here are five tests and some common sense.

Test one – look at the person selling the horse. Is

he or she neatly dressed? I don't mean they have to be in their Sunday best, but they should be neat, clean and ready to meet you. A sign of personal pride usually means they take pride in their animals.

The ranch should be well-kept, too. The barn area should be neat, clean and tidy. Equipment should be well cared for and in the proper place. Broken tools, broken fences and sloppy barns tell me the owner cares for his horses in about the same manner.

Look at the stall or corral in which the horse is kept. Wood chewers and cribbers leave telltale signs. So do weavers and hole diggers. Bad habits are hard to break. Some keep the horse skinny, and all indicate either poor training or a highly nervous horse.

The second test is to look at the horse's conformation.

If possible, have the trainer allow the horse to run free in the pasture or training ring. See how the horse uses his body. The horse should be happy to see people. He shouldn't be jumpy and he should have clear, bright eyes. I want a horse to be in good flesh, not overly fat, but definitely not skinny. Look for nice, straight legs and a smoothly put together body. There should be no sharp angles.

Most importantly, the horse's conformation should be pleasing to you.

The third test is for performance ability and training.

Of course, if you're looking at an unbroke colt, you won't be able to ride him. But you can watch the way he travels and take notice of his manners.

If the horse is broke, the owner will probably want to ride the horse and show you how well he performs. This is fine, because it gives you another chance to make some determinations about the owner.

If the owner is a bad rider, chances are the horse has had a bad start and much reschooling is ahead.

If the owner jerks, bangs, spurs and hits the horse, pack up. You don't want that bundle of trouble.

Now it's your turn to ride. The secret of a test ride is to see how slowly the horse will perform and how responsive he is to your cues.

Walk the horse, stop him, back him, jog him and lope him. Change gaits frequently and take notice of the horse's attitude about work. If he works quietly and slowly, and if he changes gaits without getting high or nervous, he passes.

The fourth test is the vet check. Don't fail to have a soundness examination. You pay if the horse passes; the owner pays if he fails.

And the fifth test is price. A horse is worth what someone is willing to pay. Usually you can get the horse for a little less than the asking price. If so, fine. If not, and the horse is the one you want, pay the price. But if a deal is offered to you suddenly, watch out. An anxious seller is a bad sign.

And, finally, this word of advice. Don't be afraid to buy the first horse you look at or the tenth, if the horse passes your test.

Along the way, you'll hear some great stories about some flashy horses, but don't change your list or requirements. Somewhere, your horse is waiting.

The White Charger

You don't pull the mask off the Lone Ranger, and you don't say Silver was a weakling or had poor eyesight.

And you don't call El Cid "babieca," which means idiot, or express doubts about the choice of horses ridden by Emperor Hirohito of Japan, or Napoleon or Gen. Zachary Taylor.

They all rode Albinos, as did many kings, queens, knights, commanding generals and Indian chiefs.

If you made disparaging remarks about their horses, you might find they didn't take it kindly, and some of them could be pretty rough characters.

But to make matters worse, you'd be perpetuating the misconception that the American Albino is weak, has poor eyes and dies young.

The true albino, which may occur in any form of animal or plant life, is a freak of nature with no color pigment. And since nature takes care of her own faults, the true albino animal is weak and does often die at an early age.

But the American Albino is not a true albino. It is instead a color type, rather than a no-color breed.

The foundation sire of the American Albino Association of Crabtree, Ore., was Old King, a horse said to be 15.2 hands, strongly built, with the necessary pink skin color, snow-white hair, and silky mane and tail. He was believed to be of Arabian-Morgan stock and exhibited great endurance and a vigorous character.

Foaled in 1906, Old King had the reputation of throwing all white foals from solid-colored mares.

The American Albino Association was actually formed in 1936 and has since established several categories for the horses in its registry.

While coloring is the primary requisite for registration, ancestry may be of any breed, Thoroughbred, Saddlebred, Quarter Horse, Morgan, Arabian, Walking Horse and light draft.

There are presently three color categories — American White, American Albino and American Creme. All have snow, or milk-white hairs with underlying pinkish skin, brown, blue, black or hazel eyes. None have pink eyes, as the name Albino would suggest. A horse is placed in one of the three color categories by making a shade of white determination — snow-white to creme (almost palomino) white. The horses range in size from the American White Pony, 12.2 hands, to 17 hands.

According to the association, the horses are exceptionally docile, smart and tractable, and are used for all types of pleasure riding, as well as for draft work and entertainment spectaculars, such as six abreast jumping exhibitions. You have, of course, seen many white horses as circus performers.

I personally don't attribute any of their performance abilities to their color, preferring to remember they are of Arab-Morgan ancestry.

Throughout history, the white horse has always been associated with the purity of the hero. White hat, white horse.

Middle Age and Renaissance painters often pictured their subjects on white horses – especially when the subjects were kings and queens.

Knights liked white horses, too, and maybe for the same reason that many cavalry commanders picked them – they are easily seen during the heat of battle, which is good for morale and as a rallying point.

El Cid chose a white horse which was scrawny, ugly and bedraggled. His choice of a horse caused people to refer to El Cid as "babieca," which means idiot. But the horse wasn't, nor, as it turned out, was El Cid. Through proper care, El Cid turned the colt into a magnificent war horse which carried his master to many victories. The final victory for El Cid occurred after he died. El Cid's embalmed body was placed erect in the saddle, and El Cid led the victorious fight against the Saracens at Valencia.

Other famous generals who rode white horses were Napoleon, who owned more than 50 of them, and Gen. Zachary Taylor, who owned only one – Old Whitey.

General Taylor rode Old Whitey throughout the Mexican War. Napoleon, however, merely sat on his white horses, all of which were trained to stand very still, since Napoleon was a notoriously bad rider. The famous picture of Napoleon on the rearing, charging white stallion was a clever effort on the part of the painter, who did not wish to upset the little general.

Mont Blanc, winner of the 1966 Woodmansterne Handicap in Epsom Downs, England, was only one of several good white Thoroughbred racehorses.

And, finally, there are the famous white horses of

American folklore, those ridden by the cowboy heroes who entertained us on the silver screen.

Hopalong Cassidy rode a white horse, but who remembers his name? Not me.

But I'll never forget the name of the Lone Ranger's horse.

"Hi, ho, Silver (Silver Pride) ... away." And the masked man rode off on the fiery horse with the speed of light.

The Name Game

What's in a name?

William Shakespeare said a rose by any other name would smell just as sweet. I also think Bill Shoemaker said that after winning the Kentucky Derby.

But I'm not convinced that applies to horses. A horse's name is something special, and he wouldn't be the same without it. It means something. It tells you about him. You can rely on it.

My first horse, Johnny One-Eye, had but one eye.

And the racehorses, Money Waster and Foolish Pleasure – those names tell you something. Would you try to ride Pecos Bill's horse, Widowmaker?

My daughter Cathy rides a horse named Sneeky Pete. Do you need to be told about his personality?

Choc's Panther.

Isn't that a great name for a reining horse? I mean, a reining horse is supposed to be "catty," and Panther, doesn't that have a feline connotation?

And a reining horse is supposed to be bold, brilliant, fast, almost dangerous. Panther. It says everything a reining horse should be.

I was looking for a reining horse prospect when I ran across Panther. He was one sick-looking cat at the time. There he stood, head down, almost licking his wounds. And wounds he had, as if he had been in a tremendous brawl in an alley at midnight.

Ann Copeland, Quarter Horse breeder who owned Panther at the time, explained he had been in race training and had flipped over, cat-like, in the starting gate. It appeared the gate had won the battle, but there was something in Panther's eye which told me he had not yet lost the war.

After a brief, but active negotiating session, Panther's registration was transferred into my name and I took him home to nurse him back to health.

The first few months were slow as Panther's left hind leg gradually mended. But as we started training for the reining class, I could almost feel a new springiness develop in Panther's gait.

At night, I was sure I could see his eyes of fire pierce the darkness. And in the morning, when it was time to work, Panther circled his corral. He was pure caged energy. As I rode him, day after day, he became quicker, striking out on the left lead, rolling back, striking out on the right lead. He barely touched the ground as he moved along. Flying lead changes seemed feline-quick and effortless.

With only a little practice, Panther could almost catch his own long, flowing tail as he spun around and around.

Yes, I knew I had a reining horse. He was quick, agile, supple, balanced, light. He was catty, that Panther.

Ten-year-old Devonne DiNicola experienced a special fascination with Panther, too. She watched us every day as I worked him. And each day, she would ask if she could groom him or give him a bath. Like any cat, Panther doesn't like baths.

I was hesitant at first. He might be just a little too much cat. Too quick, too powerful, too unpredictable, I told myself.

But Devonne's persistence paid off. I said, "Okay, but be careful." I kept my eye on their every move. Cats aren't completely trustworthy, I've been told.

Soon, I found I was saying, "Yes," to a little ride.

Again, I was cautious. "Just walk and jog," I insisted.

Now, it's just Devonne and Panther. He rubs against her, snuggles with her, longs for her gentle caress. He walks her carefully down the road, corrects his lead if she makes a mistake in cueing him, plays and frisks with kitten-like ferocity.

He likes to be with her, especially in the sun where it's warm. He snoozes while she gently scratches behind his ear.

I think he even purrrrrs.

I should have known by his name.

Panther ... you're a pussy cat!

Grab That Camera

Say "cheese." Watch the birdie!

There. Another lousy photograph of a good horse.

Why is it so hard to take a good picture of a horse? Horses are photogenic. Horses are beautiful. And for the most part, they are agreeable to posing.

The problem of course, isn't with what is in front of the camera, it's with the dummy behind the camera. Me.

To find out how to take a good picture, I talked with Kirk Willis, a professional photographer who takes hundreds of pictures of horses at shows and ranches.

The three most common problems with pictures of horses are camera angle, exposure and background, Willis says.

When taking a side view of the horse, the photographer must concentrate and focus on the natural balance point of the horse, that area just slightly behind and above the point of the elbow.

Most problems develop when the photographer is too far around toward the front or rear of the horse, or is shooting from too high or too low a position. This distorts the proportions of the horse.

The camera only records what you put in front of it,

Willis says. And a lot of bad photos are the result of poor positioning of the horse's legs.

In general terms, most breeds look best when you have the legs of the horse which are closest to the camera farther apart than the legs farthest from the camera.

"The viewer of the picture then knows the horse has four legs," Willis says. "I've seen pictures where the horse had eight legs, and that's a background problem."

Willis advises, "Don't stand the horse you are photographing in front of another horse, and try not to have a tree or pole coming out of the horse's head, neck or back. The background should be as clear as possible, especially when photographing color breeds."

Willis, who shoots for an equine photography company, says good photos of horses can be taken with almost any camera. A 35mm camera is fine and will produce good pictures if the photographer remembers to get close enough to the subject. And any of the instant box cameras work well if the photographer gives some thought to exposure and doesn't try for too much action.

"Try to photograph the horse in unobstructed sunlight," Willis adds. "Don't take a picture of a horse standing in the shade of a tree."

Early morning or afternoon sun is best, but the photographer must be careful not to get his own shadow in the picture, and if you use a light meter, use an average reading of the scene for the exposure setting. Without a meter, an excellent method is to read, then follow the instructions which come with the film.

Willis believes a film rated as ASA 64 to 25 works very well for color slides. He says Kodak's VPS film rated at 100 is good for color prints, and almost any quality black and white film will prove satisfactory.

Some pictures of horses might have turned out pretty

well but didn't simply because the animal's ears were not forward when the shutter clicked, Willis says.

The horse's ears should be up and forward, giving him an alert, interested look. Toss a handkerchief or a hat in the air in front of the horse or shake a pail full of grain, but whatever you do, get the ears up before you shoot.

Of course, the professional cameraman can improve the horse's looks with some special tricks, but so can the amateur shutterbug.

Pay attention to detail, Willis advises.

The horse should be immaculately groomed and in excellent health before you try to take a great picture.

And don't use old, broken, or dirty tack on your horse. Good-looking equipment and a good-looking rider make the horse look even better.

Get the picture? You should. It's worth a thousand words.

No Reverse Gear

John and Joy Lewis looked at me as if I were a mad man.

From their shocked expressions, I could only assume one of two things was happening. Either the horse I was backing was doing so fantastically well they couldn't believe it, or she had lost two legs and her tail had dropped off.

"Something wrong?" I asked.

In their best apologetic British manner, they hesitantly questioned my reason for backing my horse.

"To get her back," I answered.

"Oh, my goodness," said John. "I never thought of it that way. In England, horses are taught only to go forward."

Further questioning on my part revealed that only high-level dressage horses would be asked to back, and then only six steps.

A showoff might back a horse two steps just to prove he had complete control, but then, of course, he would be ridiculed for backing the horse, not for showing off.

John and Joy live in Norwich, England, and were in the U.S. on a "holiday" to see western horses.

They own and ride a horse named Lester Square. Lester is a Thoroughbred-hunter cross, 8 years old, and 16.1 hands. Lester's sire is a "premium stallion," something we don't have here, but should have. A premium stallion is selected annually for each county by the Hunter's Improvement Society, a private national organization. The society provides a grant to the horse's owner and the horse is then bred to selected mares of suitable breeding. The mare's owner does not pay the normal full stud fee.

Joy says suitable breeding today means the mare should be "a good Irish type with plenty of depth."

A similar subsidy by the various United States breed associations might discourage so many people from owning poorly conformed and dispositioned stallions, and make it possible for more people to breed to higher quality horses.

Showing in a hack class in England would be similar to showing in a pleasure class in the United States, but maybe just a bit more difficult.

Our pleasure horses are asked to walk, jog or trot, and canter or lope in both directions. They are brought into the lineup, then asked to back. The judge selects the winners.

In England, the typical hack class is judged on the horse's smoothness, lightness and manners. The riders are asked to walk, trot, canter and hand gallop. The judge then selects the top 10 horses, bringing them into the lineup. Once in the lineup, the judge may ask some or all of the riders to pull their tack. After reviewing the horses without tack, the horses are again tacked up.

Now the judge rides each horse at the walk, trot and canter in both directions. After a personal test of each horse, the judge again has the competitors take the rail, usually at the trot. At this time, the judge calls the horses into the center of the show ring in the order in which they placed.

"At times," says John, "the judge will take another look at the horse and sometimes switch a placing or two. But of course, they don't back."

I say, "Long live the Queen and the English judging system."

In England, horses are rated, and are not allowed to move to higher standards of competition until they have qualified.

Yes, it's different, but I think it makes for better horsemen — as Joy and John certainly demonstrated for me.

Our cues are different, our horses work in a different style, but neither should be considered less beautiful, less skillful, or less trained. They do different types of work, but in both cases, the training must be excellent, the cues subtle, and the responses graceful and instantaneous if the horses are to be champions.

Thanks to John and Joy, there may be a better understanding of western horsemanship in England. Certainly they have already contributed greatly to our education — and it's all been forward.

Pete Goes To The World

When you are driving 1,500 miles to a horse show, you have a lot of time to think.

The first thing you think of is, "Why, for the love of Pete, are we going 1,500 miles to a horse show?"

The answer is, of course, "For the love of Pete." Sneeky Pete is my daughter's horse, and he qualified for the World Championship Quarter Horse Show, which was held in Oklahoma City, Okla. Could we not take Pete to the World Championships? A silly question.

So along with thousands of other people and more than 900 horses, we headed across the desert, mountains, plains and prairies. Horses from nearly every state in the union were there, not to mention some from Canada and three from Italy.

Undoubtedly you are anxiously awaiting word of how Pete performed.

He performed true to his name.

Some white lines were left in the arena following the trail class and Pete, having learned safe driving habits on the trip, refused to cross any solid white line.

There were 18 horses in the class, and 14 others had a tendency to agree with Pete.

Suffice it to say, Pete is not the world champion at western riding.

But back to some thoughts about horses while traveling cross-country.

When you're in the middle of the desert and you come to a little, ramshackle dwelling 75 miles from any habitation, do you wonder why they have a horse standing in a small corral by the side of the house?

There is plenty of room to ride, true. But where are you going to ride to, or back from?

Who delivers the hay? What's the delivery charge?

Does the horse get lonely being the only horse around?

What do you do when you need a vet?

Who takes care of the horse? We must have passed a hundred or more places like that and there was never anyone around.

What does the horse think about when he's standing all alone in a trailer from 10 to 12 hours a day?

Pete was obviously bored. He managed to tear up part of the chest protection pads in the trailer and also managed to get his right front leg wrap off several times.

Apparently the water tastes different in different parts of the country. Pete liked the water in Flagstaff,

Ariz., but wasn't crazy about it in Albuquerque, N.M. The water in Oklahoma City seemed to meet with his approval, or he was very thirsty because he drank a lot.

Some competitors brought water with them for their finicky horses and changed to the Oklahoma City water gradually. I have been told a little lemon juice added to the water helps disguise the taste.

On the way, there is always the excitement of going to a new place, taking part in a new competition. There's the hope and the dreams and the plans.

Pete was excited by his new surroundings each night, but settled quickly when he discovered there were other horses about. Horses are naturally gregarious and adapt readily to new places if others of their kind are present.

Things were different on the way home. We did not experience the thrill of victory, but felt the agony of defeat. I think Pete did, too. All he wanted was to get home as soon as possible.

We were tired of sitting in a truck. Pete was tired of riding in a trailer. We were tired of eating out. He was tired of eating out, too.

We were tired of motel rooms and late to bed and early to rise. So was Pete, who likes his sleep.

As we took him out of the trailer at home, we didn't mention to Pete that he'll be going again next year.

CHAPTER II

The Human Touch

"That's one dog Slim will never get rid of at a profit," says Charlie, grinning broadly as he counts the wad of folding green once more.

"Oh," says a surprised Shorty. His grin reveals his desire to learn the details. "Did you really stick it to him this time?"

"You bet," says Charlie. He was very proud of himself. You see, hoss tradin' is kind of an art. And when it comes to buying cheap, selling high, and being gone before you turn around, Charlie is the best. And he had been trying to stick Slim with an unsalable horse for years.

Slim's philosophy has always been, "You can sell any horse. It's just a matter of finding the right person who wants that horse."

Never able to pass up a good story, I eavesdropped while Charlie and Shorty discussed the "no account, jughead" Charlie had stuck Slim with this time.

Seems as if Charlie had been trying to pick up a kid's horse at a real low price. He'd been wandering around the auction yard looking over horses when he was just about run down by a big yellow horse with four kids on his back. The kids were running him up and down the holding pens.

"Why, they had this poor old horse in such a lather, you'd have thought he'd just won the Kentucky Derby," he tells Shorty.

"So," continues Charlie, "I finds the owner and offers him $80 for the horse. He refuses, saying it's not right to sell a hoss out in back of the auction barn."

Anyway, Charlie tells Shorty, he argues with the guy for awhile but can't convince him to sell for $80. Charlie finally has to buy the horse in the auction ring, and the old yellow dog cost him $110.

"I took that thing home and put him in a pen and forgot about him," Charlie goes on. "Next morning, I go down to the corrals and I find this yellow horse stretched out on the ground, stiff as a board. I thought he was dead."

"Turns out he has arthritis so bad he can't get up until the noon sun warms his bones. Even then, it takes him 10 minutes to get to his knees, and another 10 to get to his feet."

"What did you do with him?" Shorty asks.

"I waited until late that afternoon when it was real hot, then I warmed the old horse real good and got Slim over here to look at him," Charlie replies. "You know, that old horse goes pretty good when he's heated up."

"And Slim bought him?" Shorty asked, incredulously.

"You bet," says Charlie.

"How much?" asks Shorty.

"None of your business," Charlie says abruptly, ending the story.

Well, naturally I wanted to know how Slim was making out with this old yellow cripple, so the next day I slipped by Slim's place, but there wasn't a yellow horse to be found.

"Didn't you have a yellow horse you got from Charlie?" I said to Slim, kinda casual-like.

"Yep," said Slim. "Gave $75 for him."

"What did you do with him?"

"Sold 'im."

"Had arthritis pretty bad," I said knowingly.

"Sure did," said Slim. And he was smiling.

A few days later, I'm over at Ben Williamson's place shoeing some horses when up rides Williamson himself.

"Well, howdy, Ben," I said. "Been a long time since I've seen you on a horse."

"Been five years," Ben tells me. "Last time I rode was on my 70th birthday, but I'm back in the saddle again."

"Well, that's a pretty good-looking old yellow horse," I said.

"Best buy I ever made at $150," Ben replies. "He's got arthritis 'bout as bad as me. Can't get up in the morning till the sun warms his bones, same as me.

"Every day now I go down to his pen about noon, tell him to get up, and when he reaches his knees, I just ease myself on. In another 10 minutes, he's on his feet, and we both kind of start the day nice and slow."

A Pony And A Little Love

I'm standing in the auction barn watching a young hand gee and haw a big sorrel gelding, when up saunters Slim.

The same Slim who is well known as a hoss trader of extraordinary ability. At this particular moment, he is arguing with a 5-foot, 2-inch jean-clad piece of leather known appropriately as Shorty.

Shorty says, "You can't. They aren't all that dumb."

And Slim replies in a Texas drawl, "It don't matter what they all are, it only matters that there's one.

"And it ain't that they're dumb, it's just that you've got something they want to buy."

"They ain't goin' to buy just anything that happens along," Shorty retorts.

"It don't matter what you got, if you present it right, there's always somebody that'll want to buy it," Slim says.

"I've been tradin' horses since I was old enough to chase a plow behind a mule, and I've been stuck, and so has everybody I ever knew, now, or will know," Shorty fumes, his temper beginning to show just a little. He takes a deep breath and pulls himself to full height, which means the top of his hat just about reaches Slim's shoulder. "Now don't tell me that you ain't never been took."

"Never," replies Slim.

"Don't believe it," Shorty comes back.

"Never. And never will be. With horses, there's no reason for a man to lose."

"Still don't believe it."

By now, they have shipped the big gelding, I'm engrossed in an argument that's none of my business, and the ring is filled with 20 or so wild and very woolly Shetland ponies.

The bid goes to $20 and the auctioneer says to sell 'em choice at $20 per head. Various buyers pick out the ponies they want, and soon only one is left. The one remaining has a broken leg and very little chance of finding a good home because any astute buyer knows a horse with a broken leg isn't worth much.

"I'll take him," Slim says.

Having noticed that Slim has been busy discussing some matter with Shorty, the auctioneer says, "Better look at that pony, Slim."

Slim just grins. "I'll take him for $20."

Well, everybody thinks Slim has finally been took,

especially Shorty, who can see he's won his point.

Slim puts a rope round the pony's neck, leads him hobbling out of the ring and lifts him into the back of his pickup truck. Slim, the pony and Shorty disappear into the night.

A couple of days later I read an advertisement in the classified section of the newspaper: "My name is Spunky. I'm a 37-inch pony with a broken leg. I need a home and lots of love."

Putting two and two together, I figure I've got to go out to Slim's place to see what happens.

When I pull up, there are cars, trucks and trailers parked everywhere. From the commotion and the noise, it's either a rodeo or a dog fight. In the center, I see Slim and the pony, and a sad-looking Shorty.

Slim's taking bids on the pony, and he finally says, "Sold," when a dapper-dressed fellow with a little girl hanging onto his hand says, "$50."

Soon the little girl is huggin' the pony, Slim's grinnin', Shorty's whinin', and I'm shakin' my head.

Slim says to Shorty, "Now, let that be a lesson to you.

"Never underestimate the worth of another man's horse, 'cause a horse is worth what somebody will pay for him.

"And never underestimate the power of love. It can work miracles."

And then Slim says, "If you've got any horse sense at all, you can see that losin' a little can teach you how to win."

And Shorty, he just digs in his wallet and hands Slim another $50 and says nothin'.

And Slim just grins.

Jack Remains In The Winner's Circle

"I want to go out a winner," Jack used to say.

In fact, his final request was to have his ashes

sprinkled in the winner's circle at Hollywood Park. The track management, however, refused to permit it.

Jack was a fixture on the backside of tracks all across the country, but West Coast tracks were his favorite.

"How long have you been around racetracks?" I once asked.

"My momma dropped me while she was walking hots at Saratoga," was his reply as he continued to brush the satiny sorrel gelding he was grooming at the moment.

He was a groom, a hotwalker, a barn boss, an assistant trainer, and once, a ranch manager. Jack loved his horses, though he didn't actually own any. But the way he cared for those to which he was assigned left no doubt in your mind they were his.

Jack dressed in blue jeans, a western shirt and a torn jacket. His boots were seldom shined. He often refused to shave, and he never bowed to anyone, millionaires and racetrack presidents included.

"Class will tell. You can always count on class," he used to say. "It doesn't matter whether you're talking about horses or people. I'll bet my soul on class every time."

"And how do you determine what class is?" I asked.

"You don't figure what it is," he said, plunking himself down on a bale of timothy hay.

"You just see it in a horse. Every great man and horse has got it, and you do with it, and that's what gets you to the winner's circle.

"Man o' War, Swaps, Determine . . . they all had it," he said as he pushed his back up and down on a shedrow post and smiled with the satisfaction of having conquered whatever it was that itched.

Jack had more than his share of problems, but you never heard of them from him. Troubles may have dogged him everywhere, but they never dimmed his spirit.

He never made much money. What he did make, he usually lost betting. He often owed a lot of people, but he never failed to pay.

Over the years, Jack worked for a lot of trainers, but a fella named Jerry was the one he respected most. And Jerry respected him.

They'd argue and disagree, and sometimes Jack would disappear for awhile, but he'd always come back to Jerry and a job he could count on.

"Why does Jack keep rubbing horses?" I once asked Jerry. "Surely he could do better."

"Jack's like a good claimer," Jerry replied. "He likes the company he keeps. He wins every now and then. And he doesn't want to run any faster. He knows what he can do and he does it. And just like a horse, he expects you to do the same."

As the years rolled by, most things changed, but not Jack. He was always happy rubbing horses and offering good advice: "Go out a winner."

I didn't hear of Jack's death right away, and when I did, it was in connection with the track management's refusal to grant his last wish.

A few weeks later, Jerry invited me to the races. "I've got a filly that'll win by five," he said.

Sure enough, she did.

As we started toward the winner's circle, Jerry broke into a sly grin. "Be sure to say 'hello' to Jack," he said.

It took me a moment to comprehend, and then I knew what Jerry must have done during the predawn darkness of a trainer's day.

As he had hoped, Jack would always be in the winner's circle.

Training Tips

Kenneth Boggs is conceitedly dogmatic. Maybe that's why I like him.

He isn't an average horse trainer, or an average American Quarter Horse Association judge, or an average National Cutting Horse Association judge. (He holds cards from both).

In fact, Boggs isn't average at much of anything. He's above average, or he's below average, depending upon your viewpoint. He's sometimes wrong, but more often, he's right.

Boggs says the single most important factor in training a horse is time.

"Let them alone more than you ask them," he advises. Translated, that means you show a horse what you want, then let him have time to absorb the lesson.

"Let him settle and have time to think about the performance. Horses are way smarter than most people think they are. You can bet they're a lot smarter than a lot of people who are trying to train them."

Boggs, manager of RidgeCrest Farm in Oklahoma City, Okla., cites example after example of horses burned out by trainers and riders who ask and ask and ask for an exercise the horse knows well.

"After awhile, the horse says, 'Hey, I can do it, and I've done it, and this dummy still wants more. What's the point? I'm damned if I do, and I'm damned if I don't."

"When I'm training a horse," Boggs says, "I do a lot of walking, then a lot of standing. I like the horse to have time to think about what we just did. Then," he adds, "I'll ask for a new exercise, lead changes, or something. I do a couple of lead changes — never in a figure 8 pattern because the horse starts anticipating — and then I'll just let the horse stand and think about it."

If you let the horse relax and think about what he's done, the horse begins to understand it, Boggs believes.

Boggs says he never works a set pattern.

"That just makes them sour on the whole idea. Horses get bored doing the same thing over and over, and they can't figure out the point of it.

"If I back a horse, I want him to know I backed him for a reason. If I ask for a pivot, I want the horse to see there was a reason for it. Then I let him alone to think before we go on and do something else."

Boggs has some other strong opinions.

"Thoroughbred blood is what makes the Quarter Horse good. Without it, he ain't much.

"Too many judges look for long, sloppy reins and don't understand mouth contact or leg aids.

"Too many winning show horses pull with the forehand instead of pushing with the hindquarters.

"The majority of trainers, judges and riders don't understand the bone and muscle structure of the horse. That's why some bad horses become halter champions and yet can't work."

Yes, Boggs is opinionated.

But you had better be very, very good before you challenge his opinions.

He wins a whole bunch.

Stars In Their Eyes

It seems horses get into everything, and sooner or later, it seems everybody gets into horses.

One of the early movie horse spectaculars, with a cast of thousands, involved the Greeks and the Trojans. You'll remember the Greeks hid inside a giant wooden horse which the Trojans brought inside the gates of Troy. Goodbye, Troy, hello, Helen!

There were a lot of other good movie plots along the way and in 1903, the horse really got star billing and established himself as the symbol of the western. "The Great Train Robbery" was the name of the picture, and the fast action of the horses helped create millions of loyal equine silver-screen fans.

Horses used in motion pictures are classified as extras, stunt horses, specialty actors or stars.

Horse stars such as Trigger, Topper, Fury, Mr. Ed and even Francis the Mule received royal treatment, but during early movie making, stunt horses were terribly abused.

Trip wires were attached to the front legs of the horses. They were galloped at full speed. The wires became taut, pulling the front feet from under the horses and hurtling them to the ground.

Another device was to push horses down chutes tilted over the edge of a cliff. This produced the illusion on the screen of horses falling into river canyons.

The American Humane Society put a stop to such tactics, and today, horses are trained to fall, jump and rear safely and to play dead.

Horse stars come from all breeds. Temperament and obedience are the keys in choosing the top performers. And it seems that all breeds are chosen by the human stars of the entertainment world.

Quarter Horse owners include Dale Robertson, Doc Severinsen, John Wayne, Joel McCrea and Ben Johnson.

Being a colorful guy himself, Burt Reynolds has chosen pintos, paints and Appaloosas. Colorful horses are also the choice of Slim Pickens and Richard "Shaft" Roundtree, who own Appys; Montie Montana, pintos, and Rex Allen, palominos.

Country singing star Mickey Gilley purchased his first horse, a paint, and named him Red Rose Express after his backup band.

James Brolin got into the horse business in a big way, crossing Appys with Thoroughbreds in an attempt to get some running spots. Apparently the spots were in front of his eyes too long, because it now appears he is getting out of the horse business.

Arabians are very popular with Hollywood stars. Lee Majors, James Drury, Doug McClure, John Davidson, Wayne Newton, and Sue Ane Langdon all have Arabians.

Steve Reeves has made a Herculean effort within the Morgan horse world.

Television, of course, brought the horse into everyone's living room. Television invented the rerun and the instant replay, so we could see horses coming and going.

The Appaloosa Horse Club is taking advantage of both techniques. At a recent major Appaloosa sale, the video tape replay was used to show buyers just what each horse in the sale ring was like in action.

Closed-circuit television sets were put all around the sale ring. When a horse came into the ring, potential buyers were shown a picture of the horse's talents.

For example, if the auctioneer was selling a horse supposed to be suitable for children, the spectators could see the horse in the sale ring and at the same time, watch him being handled by children via the instant replay.

At this rate, it won't be long before horses are producing and directing their own shows and movies.

With horses, things just keep improving.

CHAPTER III

Getting to Know Them

Next time you see a mule, keep in mind that but for the lack of a single chromosome and no homologous pairs, you might be looking at Secretariat.

You see, the difference between a horse and the mule is simply that the horse cells have a total number of 64 chromosomes, in 32 pairs which can be arranged in eight groups. The mule, however, has 63 chromosomes, not arranged in homologous (similar) pairs.

If Secretariat had had only 62 chromosomes, in 31 pairs arranged in six groups, he would have been a donkey.

Frankly, I didn't know that myself. But Tom Constantino, editor-publisher of Mr. Longears, the official publication of the American Donkey & Mule Society, Inc., does know of such things.

To understand more about the mule, the hinny, the donkey, or the burro, remember that Equus Asinus is an ass (or more commonly, the donkey or burro). While Equus Calabbus is a horse.

And that when you cross a male ass (jack) with a

horse, you get a mule. But when you cross a male horse with a female ass (jenny), you get a hinny.

The mule and the hinny supposedly cannot reproduce, although there are recorded cases of Molly mules having foals. Constantino says the exact mechanism involved in sterility in hybrid animals is not yet fully understood, as there are many factors involved.

There is an interesting legend about the cross which appears on the back of many donkeys and mules.

It is said that Jesus Christ rode a donkey colt into Jerusalem, and that the colt followed Christ to his crucifixion. There, the sun cast the shadow of the cross onto the donkey's back, making a permanent mark to be noted on the donkey forevermore. Mention of the cross pattern on a donkey's back is said to be found only in written works which appeared after Christ's crucifixion.

The large work mules which were so popular in America during the late 1700s and early 1800s contributed greatly to this country's agricultural success. These mules stood as high as 17 hands, and were kept as riding animals and pets as well as for pulling plows and wagons.

George Washington was not only the first President of the United States, but he was also the first recorded breeder of mammoth mules in this country. He had great faith in the draft mule and said on many occasions, "The mule is essential for America's future development."

Washington had a number of huge jackasses standing at stud at Mount Vernon. His favorite was probably Royal Gift, a large, black Catalan ass presented to him by the Spanish throne as a gift.

Everyone Wants A Champion

It's breeding season. Mare owners are seeking the

perfect stallion, and stallion owners are advertising like crazy.

What everyone wants is a champion. What everyone gets is an opportunity to pay their money and take their chance.

Genetics, or the science of heredity, is supposed to be important to the horse breeder because through the study of genetics we should be able to produce a horse which has the predictable inheritable traits we seek.

So let's make a quick study of genetics.

Horses have 64 chromosomes arranged in 32 pairs. Each chromosome carries many thousands of genes. These genes contain all the information about what the new horse will be.

Now if the genes would behave themselves, we might make a pretty accurate prediction about the new foal's inheritable traits, such as how fast the foal could run, sex, size, disposition, color, etc.

But genes are ornery little devils and they have what we call "variable expressivity." A simple example of variable expressivity is that all chestnut horses are not the same shade of chestnut. In other words, some of the genes expressed themselves a little differently.

Genes give the new foal two types of inheritance. The first is qualitative and the second is quantitative.

There are relatively few qualitative genes and lots of quantitative genes. This results in a problem, since the majority of genes, those which are quantitative, are affected by the new foal's environment.

There is a medium to high degree of inheritability in the speed of a horse, but the speed trait comes from quantitative genes, and is therefore influenced by lifestyle, food, sunshine, training techniques, and so on.

So to select the right stallion for our mare, hoping to get a very fast foal, we need to know about the quantitative genes and environments of both parents.

The stallion may have average quantitative speed genes which got a whole lot of help from his environment. Or he may have had a lot of speed from genes which weren't helped at all by his environment.

This information is difficult to acquire, but we can do several things in order to find good breeding stock.

1. Compare the records of stallions' performances. Don't worry about the pedigree of a horse further back than three generations, as the great-grandsire will have little influence on your foal.

2. Select from the very best lines. You can ignore 90 per cent of the available stallions, as they should have been gelded long ago.

3. Try to find a superior breeding animal, one with prepotency (homozygously dominant genes). How do you know if the horse has dominant genes? You'll have to check the record of his offspring for what you suspect are inheritable traits. Even then, it's just a guess.

Inbreeding, the mating of closely related animals, is a method of producing homozygously dominant horses.

However, inbreeding has its drawbacks and is not for the average horse owner.

Linebreeding is a special form of inbreeding which attempts to keep a high relationship of a single ancestor in the pedigree and can be very helpful to the average horse owner.

Outbreeding is the mating of individuals not closely related in the last three or four generations, and is probably the best system for the breeder of less than 10 or 12 mares.

Hopefully, our quick study of genetics has demonstrated the complexities of the subject. You have every reason to be a bit confused as to the results you can expect.

Based on the confusion and complexities I have wrought, the laws of probability say my recommendations should now be followed by 87 percent of the readers.

1. Select a brood mare and stallion that please you in both appearance and performance records.

2. Considering just the stallion and the mare, breed the best performer to the best performer in your field of interest. That's the law of selectivity, or your best chance for good results.

3. Understand that the study of genetics proves "what you see ain't necessarily what you get."

4. Continue to study genetics so you can be as confused and unsure as the best experts, and maybe it'll result in the much-needed further study of the horse.

Pattern Determines Color

There's always been considerable argument about the color of horses, but it's just a matter of splitting hairs.

According to Dr. Ben K. Green, the recognized authority on the color of horses, and author of a book on the subject which took 30 years to research, the color of a horse is determined by pigment patterns, not by pigment color.

To arrive at that conclusion, Green found that basically each horse has the same amount of pigment, but that each color has its own special pattern. Once he was able to recognize a particular pattern, he could tell the color of a horse by seeing only one hair.

Green says a horse hair is hollow and that the walls of the hair are clear. There is only one pigment color and that is amber.

"It is the pigment pattern and density which determine refractment of light, hence the shade of color to the human eye," he added.

Green claims you cannot predict the color of a foal. Nor, he says, has there ever been a breeding program more than 70 per cent successful in producing colors the way genetic books say they should be produced.

Green lists the following as the colors of horses: dark bay, mahogany bay, standard bay, blood bay, light bay, standard brown, seal brown, black, gray, dun, liver chestnut, dark chestnut, standard chestnut, bright chestnut, dusty chestnut, light chestnut, sorrel, buckskin, copper dun, red roan, blue roan, rose gray and grulla.

He says the only undesirable colors of a horse intended for use are the diluted colors, palomino and claybank.

There's an old saying about white feet which should tell you something about the experience horsemen have had with color over the years. It goes like this: "One white foot, buy him; two white feet, try him; three white feet, deny him; four white feet, shoot him."

White on a horse does present problems, according to Green. He says white feet are the worst to split, are softer, and should be shod if the horse is used constantly.

Of white on the hide, it is quicker to scald from sweat and heat than is a dark color, especially when the white is on the horse's face and around the eyes.

Other observations made by Green include the thought that the bay horse is the most durable, and that although cowboys brag about the dun and buckskin, you "rarely see fine breeding of a dun color."

The cowboy says the dun, buckskin or grulla are the "toughest of horses," but Green believes they simply take better care of themselves.

"These colors," he says, "belong to horses of native, western breeding. There is very little hot blood infused and self-preservation and survival are more instinctive."

Green has observed sorrels and chestnuts have more action and more speed. But, he adds, they also have a more tender mouth. And the lighter shades of chestnut have weaker feet.

A gray's skin is exceptionally tough and can stand hard use, according to Green, while the palomino has the least durable skin.

And finally, contrary to popular belief, there are more bay and dark brown Arabians than there are gray Arabians.

Much of what this experienced veterinarian has to say about color will be argued for years to come. But he has studied carefully, and who better to talk about horses in terms of color than a Dr. Green.

The Reasons For Gelding

There are too many bad stallions around. And too few good ones.

I'm not just talking about backyard stallions. I'm talking about a lot of bad stallions in the show ring, on the racetrack and at ranches.

And when I say bad, I'm not referring to disposition or manners. I'm referring to conformation and ability to perform.

Why, oh why, do so many people insist on keeping as stallions so many poorly conformed, poorly bred, tangle-footed, jug-headed slowpokes?

I won't even mention all the ill-tempered, bad-mannered studs I've seen. I blame their behavior on their handlers, even though I know some of it is hereditary.

There are three good reasons to geld a horse.

1. Bad geldings don't perpetuate themselves, while bad stallions do, thereby lowering the quality of horses.

2. Geldings are normally easier to handle and have definitely savaged fewer owners.

3. Good geldings are good for the horse business, while bad stallions are bad for business. They drag

down the price of good horses and sometimes, due to low breeding fees, keep some nice mares from going to some nice stallions.

Keeping a poorly conformed, poorly bred horse as a stallion guarantees only one thing: the majority of his offspring will be poorly conformed and poorly bred.

Usually, gelding a horse makes him easier to handle, easier to train and easier on himself. I've seen many a good stallion that would have been fantastic as a performance gelding if only his owner had shown the good sense to help him.

As a stallion, the famous racehorse Kelso was nothing. As a gelding, he was acclaimed horse of the century.

I've been told that, psychologically, a lot of would-be horsemen can't adjust mentally to the idea of gelding a horse. I believe there's some truth to it. But I've yet to meet a real horseman who wouldn't say, "Cut that horse," when he can see it is best for the horse, the breed, the owner and the industry.

I have a feeling the same psychological problem holds true in a little different way for many women owners.

I think a lot of would-be horsewomen idolize their tangle-footed, ill-conformed studs. But then, there's no accounting for some people's taste.

All this comment on stallions is the result of a simple question from Pat Miller, who wants to know at what age do you start breeding a stallion.

Dr. Kenneth G. Ormiston says breeding age depends on the individual horse, and that some horses could be used sparingly at age 2.

"However, using a young horse too often reduces his sperm count, possibly exhausting him, and possibly resulting in a less-fertile, less-healthy horse in later life."

According to Gene Cummins, Riverside (Calif.) Thoroughbred Farm manager, he would not breed a Thoroughbred before he was 4.

"Some can be bred as late 3-year-olds, but they're still growing and maturing. If they are to be bred that early, then they should not cover more than 10 to 15 mares," he says.

Norman Dunn, director of the horse program at California Polytechnic College, Pomona, says, "Whenever possible, wait until the horse is at least 3 years old." Dunn adds, "It's hard to prove that breeding at an early age has much to do with the stallion's later development, but I suspect it does."

Horsewoman Wilma Tate says, "Don't breed until the horse has been trained and worked. By that time, there's no foolishness on the part of the horse, and he's had time to grow up a little."

As for me, I believe in giving a horse as much time as possible. I'd wait until he was mature at 5 or 6.

In the meantime, he'd better prove himself superior in conformation, superior in learning ability, superior in athletic ability and superior in disposition, or I'd say, "Geld him."

Sour Horses

There are a lot of mean, nasty, sour horses in this world. They run away, balk, bite, kick, rear, strike and refuse to work.

I can accept that. I know it's a fact. But I can't accept the misplacement of blame. I can't accept the uneducated loudmouth who uses torture tactics to show the horse who's boss.

I can't accept those who, through ignorance, believe they can bribe the horse with TLC (tender, loving care). To me, TLC stands for terrible loss of control.

No, I can't allow the blame for mischief, mistakes and malice to be placed upon the horse. The blame rests solely with the owner, trainer, handler or rider, or in combination with any or all of them.

The horse is not born sour, mean or nasty. The horse is not born making mistakes in the show ring or out on the trail.

Some horses, of course, are born with less desirable dispositions than others. Some are born with less heart, less desire to please, less athletic ability. But they aren't mean, nasty or sour until someone tries to force them to meet man's warped set of standards for performance.

The horse does not perform to please man. He always reacts in a manner of self preservation. Therefore, he performs to save himself.

When a fool tries to beat, spank or club a horse into performing an exercise the horse has not yet learned, the horse simply becomes sour — biting, kicking or rearing to avoid pain and save himself.

Because the horse acts out of self-preservation, the training of horses is based on a punishment-reward system. Unfortunately, the punishment too often is overly severe and the only reward is lack of punishment.

The real art in training lies in the ability of the trainer to think before action — minimizing punishment and maximizing reward.

The great trainer guarantees the horse will get many, many more positive (reward) experiences than negative (punishment) experiences, for the great trainer knows the horse's behavior is nothing more than an accumulation of his remembered experiences.

At the same time, the good trainer does not try to bribe the horse with treats and affection. The horse will accept both, but when satisfied or annoyed, he'll do just as he pleases, unless two other elements are added. They are respect and trust.

Every good trainer wants respect from the horses in his care. Once respect is gained, the trainer uses all the time required to teach the horse the desired behavior patterns. And as the lessons progress, the horse begins to trust the trainer.

Every well-trained horse has been given time.

Every well-trained horse has respect for the trainer.

Every well-trained horse trusts his trainer.

The mean, sour, nasty horse hasn't been given time, nor learned respect, nor learned to trust.

Until we set a standard, there are no good horses and there are no bad horses.

Some horses have no trouble in meeting our standards, while others will never be able to measure up due to inherited character traits or physical ineptness. But they are neither good or bad; they are simply being judged.

When a horse performs to his maximum and his performance meets with our approval, he is called a good horse. We probably should say he has been given time, has trust and respect.

When a horse is mean, sour or nasty-tempered, he is called a bad horse. We should say he has had bad experiences.

When a horse balks, bites, kicks, strikes, rears or runs off, we know immediately he is acting to save himself from anticipated pain. We must try to find the cause of his fear and eliminate it.

The only positive cure for mean, nasty, sour horses is always the same, and it is never more punishment. The trainer must isolate the problem by returning to basic training procedures and then carefully reschool the horse, blocking out negative experiences with literally hundreds of positive experiences.

There are unskilled and unknowledgeable trainers, handlers, owners and riders who create the mean, nasty, sour horse. When they do, a good trainer, with time, can often remake the horse by the intelligent application of sound principles.

When a horse misbehaves or doesn't perform well, don't blame the horse. Understand the cause of his behavior. Remove the cause and improve the horse.

Good will overcome evil.

The Way A Horse Sees It

Horses have remarkable eyes. They can, at one time or another, and sometimes in combination, have a feather in the eye, a glass eye, a pig eye, a pop eye, a smokey eye, or a walleye.

In addition, they have both monocular and binocular vision. The horse uses monocular vision to see separate things with each eye at the same time. These objects are to the side and rear of the horse. Binocular vision, for the horse, is frontal vision, and for it, the horse focuses both eyes on the same subject.

The horse can see to the front, the side and the rear. In fact, he has a field of vision of nearly 300 degrees.

But then, the horse has a few visual limitations, too.

First, we are pretty sure the horse does not see in color.

And second, we know the retina of the horse's eye is somewhat flattened, rather than curved. This means subjects are very frequently out of focus. To bring them into focus, the horse must lower, tilt or raise his head.

The horse's eye does not focus well on subjects closer than four feet, and when a horse has his head high in the air, he cannot see the ground in front of him. Due to a special system within the eye which absorbs light rays from above, the horse cannot clearly see objects higher than his eye.

While the horse has a wide field of vision, he does have two blind spots, close to his face directly in front of him, and the width of his body directly behind him. These blind spots cause problems for both horse and man.

The horse is frightened when someone walks up directly behind him, and he is spooked when someone reaches out and pokes him in the face. Invariably that someone gets bitten or kicked.

All of the special advantages and limitations of the

horse's vision have a great deal to do with the way a horse behaves.

Just imagine what a young horse sees the first time you take him out on the trail or to a horse show.

There is the normal excitement of a strange place, cars, motorcycles, people, noises and unknown objects.

Plus there is always something happening on each side of the horse at the same time. In many cases, the action isn't in focus, and even if it was, the horse wouldn't understand it. In order to see what is going on in front of him, the horse must concentrate his full attention straight ahead. How can he do that, when there is so much new to see on each side?

Seeing is certainly disbelieving for the young horse. "How could my master have put me in such an incomprehensible world?" he must be asking himself.

Can you blame him for being a little flighty?

Many of us do, and consequently, try to jerk, spank or force the horse into calmness.

It won't work. Only understanding how he sees things will help.

And how he sees things brings us back to a feather in his eye. A feather refers to a visible blemish on the eye. The blemish may be the result of an injury or a natural defect. In either case, it is considered a fault.

A glass eye lacks color and may be cause for disqualification by some registries. A pig eye is a small, squinty eye. A horse with pig eyes is usually considered to be stubborn and hard to handle.

A pop eye is the opposite of a pig eye, and seems to be too large and protruding from the head. A smokey eye is an eye that is cloudy in color, almost smoke gray. A walleye is another term for an eye without color. It is sometimes referred to as a China eye.

Many People Get Hurt

"There never was a horse which couldn't be rode.

Never was a cowboy which couldn't be throwed."

You can get hurt around horses ... and probably will.

The first 20 or 30 times you get hurt, it'll be your fault. If you don't give up riding, the next 20 or 30 times, it'll be a chance accident. And if you still don't give up riding, the final 20 or 30 times will be the horse's fault.

Why do so many people get hurt around horses? I believe my DUDE theory explains it.

"D" stands for defying common sense. This means you wouldn't fly an airplane without some basic instruction. But the average guy who buys a horse thinks he's an instant expert just because he owns the horse.

"U" stands for uninformed. I recently taught a college course entitled "Advanced Western Training Techniques." One hundred and sixty-five persons wanted to enroll, but less than five were capable of passing the basic training requirements.

"D" stands for disrespect. Because the horse is a "dumb" animal, the owner assumes he's the intelligent one of the two. But dumb in this case means unable to speak, not less intelligent.

"E" stands for excitable. By nature, the horse is excitable, but not nearly as excitable as the dude, who comes unglued for the most unlikely reasons.

So it's not a surprise that horseback riders live more dangerously than people who participate in other athletic activities. Today's Medicine, a journal, agrees.

In 1976, the journal reported, the number of injured horseback riders rose 340 percent, while the average increase in injuries in other sports was a mere 11 percent.

Today's Medicine concluded the reasons for such an increase were the riders' "inadequate training by unqualified instructors, overestimating their own ability, plus their own foolhardiness."

The injuries sustained most often were various fractures, head and spinal injuries.

And finally, the journal reported, the equestrian death rate is 10 times higher than in other sports.

I think my DUDE theory is well-supported.

So what can be done about it . . . especially since every day more and more people are buying pleasure horses, showing horses and breeding horses?

The answer, of course, lies in the field of education.

We need more horse science programs. Only 37 major United States universities and colleges now have horse science programs, and many of these programs lack depth of subject matter when it comes to equitation and handling of the horse.

Secondly, we need to license both horse trainers and riding instructors. Trainers and instructors are licensed in most European countries, but in the United States, anyone with a horse and without a job becomes a trainer, an instructor, or both.

Every horse owner and horse lover must realize that if they studied diligently for the next 30 years, they still wouldn't know all there is to know about horses.

But we can begin by learning about the physical and psychological systems of the horse, two subjects few horsemen ever bother to study. Once we have a basis for understanding, we can go on to higher learning and greater pleasure with less accidents and injuries.

Finally, we must put a stop to the American idea that every little girl and every young horse should grow up together.

There are not many successes when the inexperienced lead, or are led, by the inexperienced.

A good, old, old horse can teach us all.

Talk Your Way Out Of This

To talk or not to talk? That's a horse-training question which has been argued for years.

Some trainers believe in talking to their horses.

Some don't. Me, I'm naturally a talker.

The horse has two physical characteristics which I believe contribute to his need for the trainer to talk to him.

The first is the horse's eyes. The horse does not see well.

But although the horse has limited vision, he has very good hearing. He has the ability to twist his ears around so he can capture sound waves. And once he does, he can distinguish between many different, subtle tones.

It is not necessary to speak to a horse in a loud voice. In fact, loud noises are irritating to him, so always speak softly.

The horse doesn't see well, and that's a negative.

The horse does hear well, and that's a positive.

Eliminate the negative and accentuate the positive, as my daddy always said, and you have a sound basis for talking to your horse.

Although the voice can be used as a training aid, too much talk can be confusing to the horse and work to the trainer's disadvantage. The trainer must be careful to use his voice as a strong cue and not as a disruptive agent.

Because I want a young horse to become familiar with my voice, I verbally introduce him to the various pieces of tack and grooming equipment we'll be using during his training. I tell the young horse how I feel his training is going and how pleased or displeased I am with his progress.

I never yell at the horse, but when I am displeased, I do speak harshly to him.

I use my voice as the major cue for performance when I longe a horse, and I always try to avoid using words which have similar sounds. I use the verbal command, "Ho," to cue the horse to stop, rather than saying, "Whoa," which sometimes sounds like "Walk."

When a horse responds properly to verbal clues, I praise him by saying, "Good boy," or "Good girl." It doesn't take long for the horse to recognize words of praise.

While I'm a believer in talk, there are those who think silence is golden.

Francis M. Ware, author of "Our Noblest Friend, The Horse," was a horseman and trainer for more than 30 years, and his advice was, "Never speak to a horse."

Writing in 1902, Mr. Ware was convinced the horse does not respond to particular words but does use the sound of the voice to recognize and identify the person.

Mr. Ware suggested there are two words, and only two words, which should be used with horses. He said, "The two words you do employ should never mean but one thing and should receive implicit obedience. 'Whoa' means stop, slide, fall or stumble perhaps, but stop dead and stand still. 'C'lk' means to proceed at once at a pace regulated by the feeling of the hand upon the mouth. The man who is eternally 'Steady, old man,' 'Whoa, boy,' or 'P-weep-p-ing' to his horse is an infernal nuisance and a menace to everyone within hearing, for he is riding every other horse in his neighborhood and spoiling the manners of his own.

"Gag yourself if you can't prevent this obnoxious habit – or buy an automobile."

Giving full credit to Mr. Ware's abilities as a horseman and his conclusions after 30 years of training, I still have to ask the question, "If two words are good, why not three, four, or complete sentences?"

CHAPTER IV

The Breeds

There's no business like show business!

At least not like the show business of James Offutt, who stood the stately, etiquette-conscious world of Saddlebreds on their high-carried tails.

In Offutt's own words: "When I was getting Montrose ready to show, I would yell for them to open the way for me. I would mount him, stick him with the spurs to raise his fire, and yell for the crowd to look out. I'd hit the ring at a dead run and race him around two or three times. Then I'd settle him and be ready to show him. All this gave Montrose notoriety."

As unorthodox as his style was, he also got most of the blue ribbons he went after.

According to Jane Burkhead Burke, secretary of public relations for the American Saddle Horse Breeders Association, Montrose was one of the most magnificent stallions ever shown. A mahogany bay, Montrose stood 15.1, unless he was in the show ring with his head and tail high. Then he measured a reported 16.2.

Maybe it was Montrose's big heart which made him appear larger, for, indeed, he had heart. At the age of 19, still entering the show ring in his special style, he gave one of the greatest performances of his life.

The Saddlebred performs in a world of his own, a world which is pretty well isolated from other breeds, for none moves as he does, nor would dare to attempt party crashing.

The American Saddlebred is a combination of English amblers and pacers crossed with horses from Spain, France, and the East.

The officially designated founder of the present type was the Thoroughbred Denmark, foaled in 1839. It should be noted, however, that the parent of the breed was the Kentucky Saddler, and that the American Saddlebred was the only horse ever to originate in Kentucky.

The speciality of the breed is its various gaits — the usual walk, trot and canter, and the artificial paces, the running walk, stepping pace, or slow rack, and the fast rack.

The Saddlebred is trained for each gait, and is known as either three- or five-gaited. The action of the gaits is high, smooth and speedy.

The rack is a single-footed pace, each foot coming down singly and with great speed, a steady 1-2-3-4 beat with no pauses.

The stepping pace is really a very old pace, with the feet on each side following each other instead of stepping diagonally, as in the ordinary trot.

While the action is dynamic, I personally can't accept it, for I believe the beauty lies in the horse's natural movement, not in an artificial one.

I can't accept the methods used to produce the action, extremely long hoofs and "soring" of the legs.

I said I was against any training methods which are cruel and painful to the horse, and I stand by my statement. And if you think it isn't common practice with 'gaited' horses, take note of this:

Within a five-day period, I received notices from the U.S. Department of Agriculture that an Alabama horse trainer pleaded guilty to soring a show horse, a Tennessee trainer did the same, and another Alabama trainer goes to trial on "soring" charges next month.

Nor can I accept the high tail carriage, which is produced by cutting the muscles of the dock and then setting the tail in position with a crupper.

No, I can't accept the fact the show must go on, regardless of the methods used. I'll accept Offutt's display of showmanship. I'll accept the Saddlebred for what he is, and I'll be happy with him without such extreme action and tail set.

So, the American Saddlebred show ring now is, for me, counterfeit. It isn't real.

Some of the sequins need to be removed. Let me see more of the horse . . . naturally.

Loyalty Can Blind

The American Quarter Horse demands a fierce loyalty from his fans.

It's a loyalty which sometimes blinds them to the facts, warps their thinking, and often keeps them from appreciating, learning, enjoying and understanding the horse.

It's a loyalty which also brings them money from breeding, showing and racing.

The American Quarter Horse, for all practical purposes, is a type of Arabian. But don't tell a Quarter Horse owner – he'll have a snit.

The American Quarter Horse isn't faster than a Thoroughbred, because he is a Thoroughbred.

The horse which carries the title, "father of the Quarter Horse," was Janus, sired in England by a stallion of the same name. The senior Janus was the son of the Godolphin Arabian (Barb), one of the immortal trio credited with the founding of the English Thoroughbred.

The junior Janus was imported to America in 1756 at a time when the horse of the day was just a little over 13 hands. Janus was a small horse himself, but he was a hand (four inches) taller than the average Virginia-bred horse.

While longer-distance Thoroughbred racing was going on in New York, short, quarter-mile racing was being held in Virginia on improvised tracks called "race paths."

Janus' physical characteristics – short, heavy and powerful hindquarters, and prominent muscles – kept him from being a good long-distance horse, but were the keys to his success as a quarter-miler. In addition to producing horses which could start fast and go fast for a quarter of a mile, he stamped his sons and daughters with his special conformation.

He was bred to many Spanish-Barb mares of the day, and soon established himself as "the quarter horse." His sons and daughters had distinctive conformation and were soon regarded as a type of horse, forevermore to be known as the American Quarter Horse.

In the meantime, quarter-mile racing was dropped for the increasingly popular long-distance racing. This, as it turned out, worked to the Quarter Horse's advantage, as he was soon adopted by the cattlemen, who loved his fast start and sprinting ability.

The combination of nimbleness and strength gave the Quarter Horse the ability to catch and hold a heavy steer, and his calmness was not affected by sudden changes of speed.

All this information is provided mainly to answer clearly the question, "How does the Thoroughbred stand up against the Quarter Horse?"

The answer is: For all practical purposes, the Quarter Horse is a Thoroughbred. They are one and the same, but they are different types, bred to do different things. And each does his thing very well.

A proposed $1-million match race between a Thoroughbred and a Quarter Horse is pointless. No matter which set of papers wins, the winner will still be a type of Thoroughbred whose founding blood comes from the Arabian.

The leading sire of running Quarter Horses is Three Bars, a Thoroughbred.

M. R. Valdez is probably the greatest stock horse trainer of all time. He rode the horse most people agree was the greatest stock horse of all time, Ebony Knight. Ebony Knight was a Thoroughbred.

I love and ride Quarter Horses. The best of their type are the best at what they do.

But I never really try to compare one breed against another.

Show me an individual horse and what he can do. Leave his papers home.

The Arabian Marvel

The Arabian horse is a marvel. How he puts up with his owners never ceases to amaze me.

Ah, but don't let me be guilty of what infuriates me so about so many Arabian horse owners — the all-encompassing general statement. I should say, "How the sensible Arabian puts up with so many senseless owners amazes me."

It is most frequently among Arabian owners that I hear the most glorious attributes heaped upon every single solitary member of the breed. It was entertainer-Arab owner Wayne Newton who made the claim that any Arabian stallion could be handled by a child.

Bunk!

There are many great Arabian horses. Arabian blood can be found in almost every finely bred horse. Arabians are noted for good dispositions, fine action, grace, beauty, endurance and heart.

But there are bad Arabians, too. Because there are bad owners, trainers, handlers and breeders.

I refuse to deny any Arabian his due, but I also refuse to excuse the bad ones.

The Arab is the father of all Oriental, or hot-blooded, horses. His purity of blood has been fanatically guarded throughout the ages, and he can easily claim to be the purest of all breeds.

Environment, of course, contributed to the evolvement of certain characteristics of the Arabian which have been sought by other breeds, therefore the infusion of Arab blood in so many useful horses. The Arab usually possesses great soundness of wind, freedom from leg troubles, great endurance, and the ability to survive under the worst conditions.

According to the American Horse Shows Association rulebook, with endorsement by the Arabian Horse Society, the Arabian type and conformation should be: comparatively small head, profile straight, or preferably slightly concave below the eyes; small muzzle, large nostrils, extended when in action; large, round, expressive eyes set well apart; comparatively short distance between eye and muzzle; deep jowls, wide between the branches; small ears, thin and well-shaped, with the tips curved slightly inwards; long, arched neck, set on high and running well back into moderately high withers; long, sloping shoulder, well-muscled; ribs well sprung; long, broad forearm; short cannon bone with large sinew; short back; loins broad and strong; croup comparatively horizontal; natural high tail carriage.

When viewed from the rear, the tail should be carried straight; the hips should be strong and round; well-muscled thigh and gaskin; straight, sound, flat bone; large joints, strong and well-defined; sloping pasterns of good length; round feet of proportionate size. The Arab's height should be 14.1 to 15.1 hands.

The Arab's skin should be dark. The color should be solid, except for legs and face, where white markings are most acceptable. White spots on the body are undesirable in breeding classes. The horse should have a fine coat.

The Arab, particularly the stallion, should have an abundance of natural vitality, animation, spirit, suppleness and balance.

Again, speaking in general terms, the list reads nearly the same as the desirable conformation characteristics of any breed. And well it should. It is when we get into specific uses for the animal that certain conformation and disposition are not desirable.

I wouldn't want to rope and jerk a 1,200-pound steer with a 14.1 Arab.

I wouldn't want to try to outrun a Thoroughbred at Hollywood Park.

I wouldn't want to try to out foxtrot a Missouri foxtrotter.

In general, the Arab is a wonderful horse. In some specifics, he's unbeatable – endurance racing, and in exclusively Arabian breed shows.

As a trail riding horse, a pleasure horse, a friend, normally he is exceptionally good. So are other breeds of horses.

As an all-around horse, he has, in my opinion, only one rival, the Thoroughbred. And the Thoroughbred is only an Arab crossed with English mares.

But every horse is an individual. Each breed has its special characteristics. Each can be praised and each can be faulted.

The Arab, unfortunately, must carry the burden of his owner.

The Arab must perform in the costume class – the costume having little to do with the horse's ability to perform, except maybe to embarrass him.

What is so highly praised, the Arab's purity of blood, is being cast aside for the love of money by the registry of half-Arabs and Anglo-Arabs.

But never fear. The Arab is a great horse, strong and with a big heart. He'll live on.

Breeders Clash Over Mustang

To most of us, the mustang is the small, swift wild horse of America.

He's the Indian pony which changed the culture of the Great Plains, making it possible for the Indian to follow the buffalo more easily, expand the area of his influence, and defeat General George Custer.

Today, he's the subject of controversy, as the battle to save the wild horse rages, and two major breed associations clash over what the mustang was and should be.

It is well-documented the mustang is tough, strong, quick and comfortable to ride.

Today, you can show him, pleasure ride him, endurance race him and breed him. And you can be absolutely positive about his size — almost.

The American Mustang Association makes 25 to 28 measurements of the mustang's body before qualifying him for registration, according to Lenore Negri, a mustang registrar.

"On size, we are absolute," she says. "The horse must be between 13.2 and 15 hands."

Then she adds, "But we are involved with a test case. The association is considering a fourth generation permanently registered mustang stallion which stands 15.1. We want to see the size of his offspring before making a final decision."

Ah, even absolutes seem subject to change.

The Spanish Mustang Registry, however, isn't ready to change its standard on size, at least not yet.

The registered Spanish mustang must be 13 to 14.2 hands in height.

According to Leana Rideout, a former secretary of the association and now an honorary lifetime member, the Spanish mustang, unlike the American always comes from the same bloodline.

"Other mustangs have been outbred to other breeds for specific purposes, but the Spanish mustang has been left alone for the last 400 years. And he is what he is," she said.

And what is he?

A descendant of the African Barb (Arabian) and the Andalusian, the original mustang was introduced to the North American continent by the conquistadores of Cortez in 1519.

If not always strong and beautiful, those horses were strong and sturdy and often quick to escape their handlers. Roaming free, these escapees formed wild bands. Many were eventually recaptured by the Indians. Constant inbreeding and a severe environment kept them at their original small size.

And the mustang registries want today's mustangs to remain small in size because the original mustangs were short.

"Just because the horses are small, it doesn't mean they are weak," says Negri. "It means they require less feed, are easier to tack up and care for. But, still, they are extremely tough."

Since the American Mustang Association still registers horses of unknown bloodlines, it relies on the 25 or so measurements to keep the conformation of the mustang much as it was 500 years ago. For example, the mustang must have a short neck, and the back can be no longer than 25 inches for mares and 24 inches for stallions, said Negri.

The original mustangs were of three basic colors. Many had a lead gray coat, black mane and tail and a dark dorsal stripe. A mustang with a brown coat was called "falgo" or "cervato." And the mustang with a light coat and reddish mane and tail was called "Navaho." Today, they come in almost every color, including pinto.

The mustang's toughness was proved many times by North America's first famous endurance rider, a Jesuit priest named Father Kino.

Although he wasn't a professional horseman, Father Kino managed to train and ride strong-willed mustangs which roamed freely over the southern Arizona desert where the padre was busy establishing missions. It is said that during the 1680s, Father Kino rode mustangs on more than 40 trips of from 1,000 to 3,000 miles each.

Spots Before Your Eyes

The words paint and pinto are synonymous, both referring to a spotted, or two-toned, horse with body markings of white and another color.

The word pinto comes from the Spanish word "Pintado," meaning colored or painted. The word paint is a slang expression of the American cowboy.

But the words paint and pinto have vastly different meanings when a horseman talks about registries.

The Pinto Horse Association of America, headquartered in San Diego, registers any horse or pony qualifying by color and conformation. The ancestry of the horse or pony need not be known, unless the horse or pony is a stallion foaled after Jan. 1, 1976. In this case, in order to be registered and remain a stallion, the foal's parents must be registered in some breed registry other than a draft breed or albino.

If the owner of a colt by unregistered parents wishes to register the colt with the Pinto Association, then the colt must be gelded to be eligible, according to Bobbi Orris, a Pinto Horse Association inspector.

All pinto horses, regardless of their ancestry, are inspected by an official association inspector. All pintos under 2 years of age are registered in the tentative division. When they reach 2, they must be reinspected and advanced to the appropriate division of the registry.

The Pinto Association is looking for three different conformation types. The most popular is the stock style, a western horse resembling the Quarter Horse.

The saddle type is more like the Saddlebred in conformation, and is stylish and animated in gait. The pleasure type has the conformation of the Arabian or the Morgan horse and is expected to be a versatile performer.

The American Paint Horse Association, headquartered in Fort Worth, Tex., is in agreement with the terms, paint and pinto, when used to describe color, but says that's where the similarities between paints and pintos come to a sliding stop.

To be registered in the Paint Association, the horse must meet size and color qualifications, but also must have both the sire and dam registered in the Paint Association, the American Quarter Horse Association, or the Jockey Club of New York, or a combination of any two of these associations.

This ruling became effective on Jan. 1, 1976. Prior to this requirement and still in effect for older horses, is a list of requirements calling for the sire to be registered with one of the three associations.

According to the Pinto Horse Association, there are more than 20,000 pinto horses registered in the United States and Canada.

The Paint Horse Association has a registry of more than 33,000 horses.

Skewbald is a term used to denote a paint or pinto which has white hair with any other color except black in the patch pattern.

Piebald, on the other hand, is a paint or pinto with white and black in irregular patches of color.

The words, overo and tobiano, refer to the two paint or pinto horse color patterns. These patterns can be distinguished by the location of the white on the horse. While there are certainly exceptions to practically every rule for identifying these patterns, the following guidelines are pretty accurate.

The overo often has jagged, or lacy-edged, white marking, mostly on the midsection of the body and neck area. The white rarely crosses the backline, from the withers to the dock of the tail. The legs are usually a color other than white.

There is more variation of pattern with overos than with tobianos. Most tobianos have color on the head, chest, flanks, and in the tail. The legs are nearly always white, and the white markings extend over the back. The edges of the markings are usually fairly smooth and rounded.

Now we know if the horse is piebald, skewbald, overo or tobiano, but to determine if the horse is a paint or a pinto, don't look at the horse.

Look at his papers.

Pinto Has Its Own Hat

Some horses wear hats – naturally. And while the hats don't keep the sun off their heads or shade their eyes, they do make the horses "invincible."

The hats are really a color pattern on pintos, and the horses which wear them are called Medicine Hats by the Indians, and pinto and paint owners and breeders. By those who fought the Indians, the distinctive marking was called a war bonnet.

According to Sylvia M. Schell, who is a breeder of paint horses, the Plains Indians favored the pinto horse because he added color to their ceremonies and he carried his own natural camouflage. And the most prized pinto was the Medicine Hat pinto.

The true Medicine Hat pattern is really two patterns in one, Schell says.

First, the horse must have a dark color which covers only the ears and top of the head. The remainder of the head is white. In addition, the horse must have a color pattern in the form of a shield on its chest.

The Indians thought the shield protected the horse's chest and made the horse and rider invincible. Only the braves who had proved themselves were allowed to ride a Medicine Hat horse into battle.

While the Medicine Hat and the shield are simply color patterns, it seems the blood of these horses runs particularly hot, and from recorded events, it appears they had great courage, Schell says.

The Cheyenne, Sioux, Blackfeet and Comanche possessed these sacred horses in great numbers during the 1860s, Schell says, and were doing quite well in their battles with the white settlers and soldiers.

Another unusual aspect of the Medicine Hat horses is that although their legs are usually solid white, their hoofs are black or striped, she says.

And what is a Galiceno?

A small, easy-moving, tireless horse which is rapidly becoming very popular in the United States.

Thought to have originated in Galicia, a province in northwestern Spain, the breed is believed to have been in existence even before Columbus almost sailed off the edge of the earth.

Experts say the Galicenos were among the first horses landed on the North American continent when Cortez invaded Mexico from Cuba in 1519.

Today, there is an association of Galiceno breeders and there are special Galiceno breed shows in which the horses are asked to perform pleasure, stock and western riding routines.

Once the horse of the Conquistadors, the Galiceno is quickly making a name for itself as the horse of the competitors.

Peruvian Paso Excels

I like Verne Albright. I don't know him personally, but I like him. I like the way he thinks.

Verne says the Peruvian Paso is probably the "least versatile horse in the world." And that has to be a very honest statement coming from the man who is called Mr. Peruvian Paso.

Verne has confidence in the breed of horses he's

chosen, so he doesn't try to please everyone by making outlandish claims for the Paso. Verne Albright says simply that what the Paso does, he does better than any other horse in the world. He's the absolute master.

What does he do and what is he like?

"The Paso is the best trail horse in the world and the best for just plain pleasure riding," replies Albright.

You don't make a stock horse, reining horse, or cutting horse out of the Paso, Albright admits. You just ride him and enjoy it, he says.

Albright is secretary of the American Association of Owners and Breeders of Peruvian Paso Horses, and editor of The Peruvian Horse World, the association's official publication.

An expert on the Paso, Albright says this naturally gaited (style of movement) horse is descended from bloodstock introduced into Peru by the Spanish. The horse has the blood of the Barb, the Friesisan, the Spanish Jennet and the Andalusian.

At the beginning of the 17th Century, the most popular horses were gaited, according to Albright. Their smooth performance was highly regarded by those who had to ride astride in order to travel.

But by the close of the 17th Century, when the buggy was introduced, the gaited horse was out and the trotting horse was in. Horse racing had also gained worldwide popularity, another activity not suited to the gaited horse.

The Peruvians didn't care, however, and kept right on breeding the gaited Paso.

For several centuries, no outside blood was introduced into the breed, says Albright, and now the Paso is the only naturally gaited breed in the world which can guarantee passing its gait on to 100 per cent of its offspring.

The Paso's inborn gait is a four-beat lateral gait, and is, without argument, the smoothest in the world.

In addition, the Paso is the only horse in the world with "termino," which is a graceful, flowing movement in which the forelegs are rolled toward the outside as the horse strides forward. Termino is a spectacular and beautiful natural action.

The Paso's gait can be as slow as a walk or as fast as an extended trot or slow canter. Mounted on a Paso, the horseman is motionless in the saddle and his head always stays level.

With the Paso, no special training or artificial devices are used to aid the gait. The horse is shown without shoes and with a short, natural hoof.

The Paso comes in all basic solid colors, stands between 14 and 15 hands, and normally weighs between 900 and 1,100 pounds, about the same as a Morgan or Arab.

At the present time, there are approximately 1,400 Peruvian Paso horses in the United States and no more than 5,000 in the world.

I congratulate the Peruvian Paso breeders and owners. They know what their horse is and does, and they like it that way.

And I predict the Paso will be the hottest breed in the nation for the next several years.

Return Of The Shire

The magnificent shire has staying power.

He outlived the knights and their shining armor.

He gave way gracefully to the motorcar. And watched with a calm and knowing eye as the streets and highways of Britain rapidly filled with choking, smoking, noisy, costly traffic. He maintained his gentleness, beauty, dignity and patience as the British dray (a flat deck cart with four wheels) sat idle, gathering dust.

He would be needed once again.

And so he is.

Today, the sight of the brewer's dray, loaded with good British ale and pulled by a pair of massive shires, is back on the streets of England. And, as in the days of old, the shire is reasserting himself on the British farm.

My friend, John Lewis of Norwich, England, says the shire's return to glory is just plain "horse sense."

As John explains it, inflation and hard times have everyone cost-conscious. And the English brewers were the first to do some hard thinking about the cost of delivery.

A truck costing $10,000 in England has a useful life of about six years. A gallon of diesel fuel costs $1.60, and the truck gets only eight miles to a gallon. To make matters worse, the cost of repairs and parts is exorbitant.

The final blow to the truck was the fact that most of the time it sat, motor running, in a traffic jam.

On the other hand, John says, two good shires cost about $3,500, have a useful life of 15 years, make the same speed in town as a truck, and only cost $14 a day to feed.

The shire has been returned to the farm, John adds, for reasons of economy and efficiency. Tractors are expensive, shires less costly. And when the tractor gets stuck, the shire plods on by. He can pull up to five tons.

Actually, John says, the British have found the shire does a better job of plowing in certain soils by not compacting the dirt so much and providing a better distribution of soil.

Americans are catching on to the value of shires. For years, they have been used in the United States as logging horses, but now buyers, mainly from Texas, the Midwest and the Northwest states, are going to England to buy shires. "And their interest has hiked the price nearly tenfold in recent years," John adds.

The shires appeal to U.S. buyers because, like the

Quarter Horse, they are built to work and have a kindly temperament to match their stamina.

The shire is the biggest, broadest horse in the world. The shire at maturity weighs a ton or more and stands at 17 hands. A mare is usually just a bit smaller. Termed the "traditional British horse," the shire is descended from the great horses of Belgium crossed with English mares.

In addition to his size, the shire is distinguished by the feathering which adorns his legs.

The feathering normally begins just below the knees and hocks and is full and heavy. It often gives the shire the appearance of wearing bell-bottomed pants. And the feathering is functional. The shire is raised in the marshy fen which is covered with sharp-bladed sedge grass. The feathering keeps the horse's legs from being cut by the grass and keeps the dampness of the marsh from his heels.

The shire's predominant colors are bay and brown, then black, then gray. In most cases, the shire has some white markings on the face and legs.

John says the shire was called upon once before when England had gasoline troubles.

During World War II when fuel was available only to essential users, hundreds, indeed thousands, of shires were used on farms and to deliver coal, bread, vegetables and general cargo in towns and cities.

Yes, the shire has staying power. It appears he may be in Britain to stay and here to stay. Gasoline prices just went up again.

The Pride Of Russia

I have always subscribed to the theory that, essentially, the Arabian is the oldest breed.

Not so, say the Russians.

"There is historical evidence to the effect that the Akhal-Teke breed is much older than the Arabian," according to officials at V/O Prodintorg, a Moscow import-export company specializing in racing, breeding, draught and meat horses.

The Akhal-Teke was originally of Turkmenia, where it was bred for centuries without mixing with other breeds. Finally exposed throughout Russia and Western Europe, the breed has performed extremely well and is considered among the world's best sport horses.

The horse is similar in conformation to our own Thoroughbred, except it is a little lighter. This lightness is probably due to the environment of the land where the horse originated. Southern Turkmenia (on the Russian border adjoining Iran and Afghanistan) is desert. The Turkoman tribesmen tethered their horses most of the time, hand fed them a mixture of lucerne and barley, and were extremely demanding when asking the horses for work.

Today, the horses possess great speed for both long and short distances, have good jumping ability, fiery but submissive temperaments, and recover quickly from strenuous activity.

In conformation, the Akhal-Teka is noted for its small, light head with large, expressive eyes, a long, thin and yet muscular neck with almost no mane, long, refined legs with clear-cut tendons, and very sensitive, smooth skin with short, glossy hair. The most desirable Akhal-Teke color is pale honey gold.

The most famous Akhal-Teke was the stallion Absent. Under the Russian rider Sergei Filatov, Absent won the title of Olympic dressage champion.

Other Russian horses include the Tersk, which was developed by crossing Thoroughbreds and Arabians at the Tersky and Stavropolsky breeding centers.

The Tersk is somewhat larger than the Arabian, but differs little in other characteristics. The horse has a clearly pronounced Oriental appearance and is well-proportioned. The horses are used in competitive sports such as dressage and hunting, and are popular as circus performers. They also do well in long distance racing.

The Trakehner breed derives its name from the Trekehner stud, catalogued in 1732, according to Prodintorg. Again, this horse is a cross of Thoroughbred and Arabian, as well as some Akhal-Teke breeding. In Russia, the Trekehner horses are used in obstacle races and steeple chases since they are large and have good bones and fine, dry joints.

Riding Pepel, a Trakehner stallion, Yelena Petushkova became world champion and a silver medalist at the Munich Olympics.

If you want to ride in the mountains, the best horse is the Kabarda, suggests Prodintorg. The Kabarda is a strong, persevering and unpretentious horse with a quick trot and gallop. The Kabarda is the result of a complex crossing of Turkmenian, Arabian, Nogai and other breeds of the Northern Caucasus. They are distinguished by their medium-sized head with a characteristic "hook" nose profile. They also have very hard hoofs which make shoeing unnecessary.

Of all the Russian horses, my favorite is the Don horse.

Bigger and heavier than our Thoroughbred, but with much the same conformation, the Don horse has a small head, muscular neck and short, strong back. The Don breed developed in the 18th-19th Centuries in herds which belonged to Don Cossacks. The horses were bred through a long process of complicated crossing of the local horses, originally from Mongolia, with Turkmenian, Arabian, Persian, Karabakh and, later, with Orloff-Rostopchin, Strelets and Thoroughbred horses.

They are strong, persevering, unpretentious and good-tempered horses which move very well at the trot and gallop, boldly taking any obstacle. The Dons are chestnut or brown, but always with a golden hue.

CHAPTER V

Care and Feeding

It's foaling time. Ah, the joy of being a new parent. Even if that funny, long-legged baby does have silly, crooked whiskers.

The birth of a foal is a beautiful and exciting experience, but there can be danger, too.

Understanding the foaling process eliminates some of the dangers, while unskilled or untimely assistance increases the chances of disease, or even death for the foal, the mare, or both.

Dr. R. J. Brown, D.V.M., of Norco, Calif., suggests you do little to assist nature at foaling time.

"Nature does a pretty good job on her own," he says. "And in too many cases, an overly helpful owner creates problems where there were none."

He recommends you have three things on hand at foaling time: 1. A bottle of iodine. 2. Some clean towels. 3. A clean, dry, sheltered area for the mare and foal.

The iodine is to be poured on the foal's navel cord just after the cord breaks. This is extremely important, since navel infection is common among foals. The cord represents a direct passage to the foal's bladder and to the blood supply to the liver.

Any infection which gets into this passage is transmitted to the rest of the foal's system and easily can result in Joint, or Navel Ill, a severe disease which can cause death.

The clean towels are used to dry the foal after birth. It isn't necessary that you do this, but in cold weather drying the foal keeps it from becoming chilled and gets the little one's circulation going.

If the weather is nice, the best place for the mare to foal is a grassy pasture. But if you want the mare sheltered, be sure to put her in your biggest stall. Both straw and wood shavings make good bedding for the mare and foal.

Now that you're prepared, let's check the sequence of events.

The average pregnancy is 342 days, give or take 10 days. As foaling time approaches, look for telltale signs. The mare's milk glands will enlarge and a waxy substance may develop on the ends of the nipples.

Milk may drip or stream from the nipples, a good indication foaling will occur within 15 minutes to 48 hours.

As the time nears, the mare will exhibit nervousness, showing all the signs of colic for, indeed, she does have stomach cramps.

The water bag will appear and break. Don't be concerned, as there will be lots of water. In 15 minutes or less, the foal's front feet should appear. In a normal birth, the foal's head will be between the front feet. It is not uncommon for the mare to get up and walk around before the birth is complete. From the time the feet first appear, it will take from two to 10 minutes for the remainder of the birth process.

Let a normal birth take place, advises Brown.

Your main job as the observer is to look for signs of an abnormal birth presentation.

If anything other than the two front feet and the head should appear, or if nothing appears after 15 minutes of hard labor, call your vet, describe exactly what you see and follow his instructions carefully.

If the sack is still over the foal's head after the birth process is complete, stick your fingers through the membrane at the foal's mouth, then pull the sack back away from his nostrils so the foal can breathe. Don't do anything else until the mare has cleaned the foal and both have relaxed. Then put iodine on the foal's navel cord and rub the foal with the clean towels.

It will take from five minutes to three hours for the mare to expel all the afterbirth. Collect the afterbirth so it may be checked by the vet.

When the foal decides it's time for a drink, he'll try to get to his feet. This can take from 15 minutes to an hour, and you'll want to ease his struggle, but don't. The exercise is good for the foal.

The foal should be nursing within two hours. If he isn't, then a little assistance may be helpful. But don't try to push the foal toward the mare. He won't go. Stand on the opposite side of the mare and try to get the foal to suck on your fingers. Then guide him toward the milk. A squirt on his nose will get his attention.

The foal should pass the meconium from the rectum shortly after having a good drink of milk, says Brown. If the foal shows signs of straining, tail elevation or cramping, call the veterinarian. Do not give the foal an enema yourself.

Within 12 hours of foaling, have your vet check both the mare and foal and administer disease-preventing medication to both.

As simple as it is, that's the wonderful miracle of foaling.

Getting In The Swim

Hot, bright sun. Long summer days. Perfect for

taking a dip in the cool, sparkling water of the backyard swimming pool.

Horses are doing it by the thousands.

But swimming is nothing new for horses.

The horse soldiers of the Roman Empire swam their horses, and so did the armies of the Napoleonic era. The American Indians even invented water games on horseback.

As in the past, however, most of the horses who swim today do it for its therapeutic value, not for fun.

Swimming is good for humans and for horses, too.

"You take an old, tired, sore horse and give him a vacation around the pool, and in two or three weeks, he'll be prancing and dancing," says Larry Heineman, manager of El Rancho Murrieta, Murrieta, Calif.

And it's a good way to condition a horse, he adds. The horse has to extend himself to stay afloat. That means he uses all his muscles, his heart and his lungs.

According to Heineman, backed up by a number of published medical reports on the swimming of horses, a horse which is swimming will be ready for the race track as much as 30 days sooner than the horse which just gallops on the track.

"Swimming isn't a complete substitute for galloping," Heineman says. "A horse has to have the experience of running on the track, too."

Swimming therapy works best on horses which have been injured and can't stand the strain of galloping, but still need to be kept in shape.

"Swimming gives them the exercise they need but doesn't punish them as much as running," he explains.

The pool at El Rancho Murrieta is 13 feet deep and 40 feet across. It is shaped like a doughnut, with an island in the middle instead of a hole.

The secret to swimming a horse is having good men work with the horse, Heineman says. A horse won't necessarily extend himself, or sometimes he's afraid and he panics, so the handlers have to know how to get him in the water and how to work him so the exercise does him some good.

At El Rancho Murrieta, the horses are led into the water down a gradually sloping chute. A man is stationed on the island and another on the outside edge of the pool. They keep the horse safe and swimming. One lap around the pool takes one minute.

Heineman says he starts horses out by swimming them three to five laps the first few days, and over a period of time, works them up to 18 minutes a day.

Most horses swim naturally, but just like some humans, some horses never get the hang of it. If they don't swim, they sink.

"I had one horse which went into the water all right. But once in, he just rolled over and sank, with his feet going under last. We saved him, but it was close," Heineman says.

Some horses won't work at swimming. Heineman tells of one horse which would take several strokes, then relax, just letting himself slowly sink. Just before his nose went under, he'd stroke again.

"He was just a pool bum," Heineman adds.

While swimming horses as therapy was very big a few years ago, its popularity has declined in recent years, as the big pool has been replaced by the therapeutic whirlpool spa.

Promoted by East Coast horseman Robert Leonaggeo, the whirlpool spa provides the horse with a gentle massage of legs, shoulders, back, loin and hips.

Leonaggeo says it's fantastic for the leg-weary horse or the horse suffering from minor aches and pains. And to make the whirlpool even more delightful, the water is heated.

But pool or no pool, kids and horses will be swimming in ponds, lakes and rivers all summer long.

Some safety tips: Be sure your horse can swim before you turn him loose. Never get in front of a swimming horse. He's liable to swim right over you.

Hang onto the horse's mane so you don't interfere with his head.

Finally, horses are easily embarrassed. Don't ask one to wear a bathing cap and water wings.

Flies In The Ointment

Flies. I hate them.

They're nasty, annoying, dirty, pesky and a tremendous bother, both to me and to horses.

But what to do about them? Commercial fly sprays don't seem to work very well. The flies become immune to them or the wind blows the spray away before it kills the flies. Wipes work for a short period of time, then do no good at all. Some wipes, if used often enough, actually cause the horse's hair to fall out, while others are irritating to the horse's eyes.

The best advice I've found so far is the fly swatter. When you smash one of the pesky little devils, he doesn't bother you any more. His friends do.

Robert H. Soroker, R.S., public health entomologist for the Division of Environmental Health in Riverside County, Calif., says the best approach to the fly control problem is the educational one.

He is convinced that flies on a horse ranch can be virtually eliminated, or at least reduced to a very low level.

The answer, he says, is breaking the life cycle of the fly.

Flies need three conditions to breed. Food, moisture and warm temperatures. The horse provides the first two and the sun provides the third.

In her lifetime of from two weeks to two months, a female fly can deposit from a few hundred to two thousand eggs. The eggs hatch into larvae, which then feed on organic matter and in a short time, grow into pupae, which then change into adult flies, which repeat the cycle.

In order to break this cycle, you must start, and continue, a fly control program, says Soroker.

He suggests:

Construct box stall floors of material which will prevent fly breeding, such as compacted clay or compacted soil.

Bedding material must be kept clean and dry. Soiled bedding and manure must be removed daily.

Remove manure at least twice a week from all stables, paddocks, exercise areas and training rings. Pay particular attention to manure which accumulates along fence lines and around water troughs and feeding areas. Dispose of manure in fly tight bins, or spread it so it dries quickly.

Keep feed storage areas clean.

All water troughs, bowls and other water sources should have a non-leak valve so the ground around them stays dry.

All ponding or water collection areas should be regraded or filled in so there are no wet, muddy areas. This is especially important in stalls.

Soroker says the most common fly breeding areas on horse ranches are wet piles of manure or organic materials such as moist food, wet ground around watering areas, and piles of hay and manure.

The housefly and the biting stable fly are the two most common flies around horses. The housefly is simply a pesky, dirty critter which lands on things and bothers you. The biting stable fly does just that . . . to both man and horse.

If you eliminate horse ranch flies on your own ranch, as Soroker says you can do, what about the flies created by other horse ranches and poultry ranches nearby?

If you have a lot of flies hovering in shaded areas, they are probably from neighboring poultry ranches, which could be as far away as four miles or even 20 miles.

To protect your horses from flies from other ranches

(after you have taken steps to eliminate flies at home) you might try feeding them brewer's yeast.

According to Robert Dorotik of Laytonville, Calif., writing in Prevention Magazine, brewer's yeast fed to horses will keep the flies away from the horses.

There is no explanation yet as to how or why the brewer's yeast works, only the affirmative observation that it does work.

Dorotik reported a virtually fly-free condition around his horses after feeding them brewer's yeast for 30 days. He said he used two tablespoons of brewer's yeast per horse every two or three days. You can purchase brewer's yeast at the local health food store.

Dorotik said he also tried torula yeast and got the same results with the same dosages and at a reduced cost. He said he buys torula yeast in bulk for 70 cents a pound.

I'm trying both Soroker's fly control program and Dorotik's brewer's yeast cure.

I have tried cider vinegar, and while my daughter Cathy says she believes it did keep the flies away from the horses, I'm skeptical.

But if you wish to feed your horses cider vinegar, use about a quarter of a cup each day and invest in a fly swatter.

A Balanced Diet

The average horse owner doesn't know what or how much to feed his horse.

But, then, neither does the expert horseman.

The simple truth is no one knows exactly what, nor how much, to feed a horse.

According to most veterinarians who treat backyard horses, underfeeding is common.

But go to a major horse show and the situation is just the opposite — too many overfed horses.

I have discussed feeding programs with dozens of

nutritionists and the conclusion is always: "We just don't know all the answers."

However, we do know something about what horses eat. They eat everything from coconuts to dried fish. Over the last 50 million years, they have done well on grasses and hay and a variety of grains but, then, most of the time they were running free, not at the mercy of a captor.

There is no way the average horseman can run tests for nutrition on every bale of hay or every sack of grain fed. To some extent, though, we can rely on the feed manufacturer and the hay dealer to provide a fairly good quality of feed. And if we feed the hay and grain by weight, we can be pretty sure the horse is getting sufficient amounts of protein, carbohydrates, vitamins and minerals.

Most nutritionists recommend the horse be fed about two per cent of his body weight in good hay and grain. (An 800-pound horse would get 16 pounds of feed per day.) This daily ration should maintain a mature horse doing light work of one to three hours per day.

Be sure the horse has access to a salt block and plenty of clean, fresh water.

The ratio of hay to grain can be started at four parts hay to one part grain and changed if necessary, depending on the horse and how well he does, for this is the final test of good nutrition.

What about supplements?

Supplements won't hurt the horse, and they can be a form of insurance to make sure the horse gets a complete diet.

But if the supplement is fed to promote rapid growth or put on large amounts of weight, it can be dangerous.

"Excesses of vitamins and minerals can, at times, be damaging to the horse's well-being," says Dr. Tony J. Cunha, dean of the School of Agriculture at California State Polytechnic College.

The horse has a built-in timer which tells him when he should be fed. Being a creature of habit, he doesn't like his meals served early or late. He would also rather have a smaller breakfast and a larger dinner, so one-third of his ration should be fed in the morning and two-thirds in the evening. Feeding three times a day is even better if it is convenient.

The method of feeding is also important.

Feeding on the ground is dangerous and wasteful because the horse picks up dirt and sand and loses the best part of the hay, the leaf.

Overhead feeding racks are unnatural for the horse. They are frequently the cause of injuries to the horse's eyes, either from hay dust or from the feeder.

A grain-tight manger is best. It should be three and one-third feet off the ground at the top and at least two feet wide at the top.

Until we know more about diet and the horse, we must do the best we can, neither underfeeding nor overfeeding.

And we should keep asking questions about nutrition so research will continue and more answers will be found.

Until then, ask your horse. An eager eater who is getting enough good hay and good grain will look, act and feel like a good friend.

Colic Can Kill

Colic is a killer, yet it isn't a disease.

It's a stomach ache — horse size!

Colic is the name we give to any abdominal pain the horse suffers until that pain is specifically diagnosed. In many cases, the horse is treated for colic and the real cause of the trouble is never investigated.

We could reduce the number of stomach aches significantly if we wormed our horses regularly. According to a report by the American Association of Equine Practitioners, "90 per cent of all colic cases result from damage done by bloodworms."

In order to prevent the other 10 per cent, we'll have to look for other colic causes.

Colic can be caused by a sudden change in feed. Horses should be introduced to new feeds gradually, especially lush, green feeds.

Poor or moldy feed can cause colic, as can an irregular and sporadic feeding schedule. Establish both the amount you feed and the time you feed your horse and then stick to the schedule.

Just as with people, colic can be caused by overeating, or the overeating can cause gas, which results in colic. And it doesn't matter how you spell relief, the product isn't available to the horse.

To make matters worse for the horse, unlike a lot of human overeaters, the horse has a very difficult time burping, or he's just too polite.

Other contributors to colic are cribbing, too much water after a hard workout and poor teeth, which keep the horse from chewing his food properly.

A common cause of colic is sand impaction, which means the horse has ingested sand with his food. Do not put your horse's feed on the ground, and be sure the horse is getting enough to eat so he isn't sifting through the soil looking for a stem of hay.

No matter the cause, the signs of colic include restlessness and sweating. A colicky horse will often pace or paw the ground, and frequently he will break out in a mild or sometimes heavy sweat.

If you ask your horse what's bothering him, he'll often look at his sides, or he'll bite at his sides or rub his sides against the wall or fence. If your horse is in severe pain, he may even kick at his sides.

Certainly the horse with colic will not eat and most likely will not drink. He may moan a good deal, and if you put your ear to his side, you'll hear a lot of stomach noise. There are, of course, normal stomach noises, but they are not usually as persistent or as loud as colic noises.

Finally, the colicky horse will frequently throw himself about in agony. He may get down and roll, which can result in a twisted intestine, almost always fatal.

If your horse shows any of these signs, act immediately. Call your veterinarian.

The call may not be necessary, as the colic may disappear on its own, but it's always better to be safe than sorry.

The veterinarian may ask what you have been feeding, how long the horse has had the symptoms, when he was last treated for worms, and what recent activity the horse has had. Be sure you are ready with the answers.

You should then follow any advice the veterinarian gives.

While you are waiting for a veterinarian, do not let the horse get down and roll. It is best if you walk or jog the horse. This may help relieve a gas pocket, which may be the cause of the colic. Don't overexert the horse, however. The idea is to relax him, not make him tired.

If you can't reach a veterinarian, or feel you must take immediate action, then you may try to give the horse a pint of mineral oil mixed with one tablespoon of turpentine every hour.

This acts as an anti-ferment to relieve some of the gas and loosen an impacted bowl.

But, again, I caution you, colic is a killer.

When a horse has a tummy ache, act quickly and get professional help.

The Enemy Within

While the chances of ridding your horse of worms are slim and none, the chances of your horse dying from worm-related problems are good and very good.

According to Dr. John B. Herrick of Iowa State University, more than "50 per cent of all horses die directly or indirectly from internal parasites."

Actually, you don't need to know what to look for to determine whether or not your horse has worms. I can assure you he does. However, the most noticeable external signs are rough hair, a pot belly, fever, coughs, listlessness, diarrhea, dull or watery eyes, and poor growth. Any of these signs, alone or in combination, indicate the worm problem could be severe.

But even if your horse has a shiny coat, is fat and appears to be quite healthy, the horse probably is infested with worms. Several different studies of parasite infection show the average horse carries more than 30,000 worms and bots.

Of the five common types of worms, two are bloodworms, probably the most devastating parasite to the horse.

Strongylus Vulgaris gets its name, bloodworm, because as an adult, the worm sucks blood after it attaches itself firmly to the walls of the large intestine. It is while the bloodworm is attached to the walls of the intestine that the female deposits a large number of eggs, which pass with horse droppings to the ground.

Once on the ground, the worm larvae hatch, then fasten themselves to grass, which the horse eats. Back inside the horse, the larvae migrate for about six months before returning and maturing in the intestines to reestablish the cycle.

The large bloodworm attaches itself to the intestine wall, sucks blood, can block the flow of blood and damage artery walls.

Small bloodworms burrow into the intestinal lining, causing ulcers and interfering with digestion.

Bots, a fly larvae, damage the horse's tongue, lips and throat, as well as interfering with digestion once they have attached themselves to the stomach wall.

Roundworm larvae will migrate throughout the horse's body, penetrating the intestinal wall, the liver and the lungs. They are especially dangerous to young horses. They can grow to be a foot in length and can block the intestine or puncture it.

Pinworms in large numbers can upset the horse's digestion and sometimes cause anemia. They are often the cause of "tail itch."

Owners should give special attention to new foals, as roundworms will severely retard the absorption of needed nutrients, which in turn stunts the foal's growth. The roundworms may even block the foal's intestines, causing death. This can, and has, happened to foals as young as three months.

Worms are a problem all year long and are virtually impossible to eliminate because of the structure of their life cycle.

Having a horse wormed by tube or other method kills most of the adult and immature worms. However, there are still thousands of eggs remaining in the horse and ready to hatch at different times.

In addition to the eggs, the migrating larvae, which move through the horse's body for six months or longer, most likely will not be affected by the medication. The larvae become adult worms, which lay more eggs, while the other eggs are passed out of the horse, then reswallowed to become new larvae.

To make the battle even rougher, a single horse with an average worm infection, may be depositing up to 25 million new eggs each day in his manure. The results are obvious.

If everything you have read so far is scary, give some thought to this. The majority of horse owners don't know as much about worms as you have already read. And nothing I know is worse for a horse than an owner who doesn't have a basic knowledge of horse health and care.

But don't panic. There's a lot you can do to minimize the parasite problem.

Because the life cycle of the worm is continuous, any worming program must also be continuous. Get the advice of your veterinarian and begin a regular health program immediately. Don't miss a single horse, no matter how healthy he appears.

Many vets recommend tube worming twice a year, usually around the first of June and the first of December. In addition, they usually recommend you add a wormer to the horse's feed about every eight weeks.

There are a number of good feed additive wormers available at feed and tack stores, or from your veterinarian. Keep records and administer the medications on schedule.

If your horse is finicky and won't eat the medication in his grain, try adding a little molasses, just enough to disguise the taste and hold the medication in the grain.

Or you can try raspberry-flavored Jello. Many horses love the taste of raspberry.

Several days before you plan to add the wormer, mix the dry Jello with your horse's feed. On the third or fourth day, add the wormer and the Jello and watch him become a happier, healthier horse.

Tetanus Danger

I got bit by a horse.

He was a nice horse until he bit me. Then he was a mean, nasty, bad stallion, and I told him so.

The bite broke the skin and the wound bled, then turned a nice deep purple.

Did I need a tetanus shot?

Every horseman should know the answer, but few do. I didn't, so I decided to ask members of my equestrian college class of more than 30 people.

"You need a tetanus shot every year," one said.

"No, you don't," said another. "You'll be all right. Don't worry about it."

A young woman said, "If the bite broke the skin, you'll have to take the painful Pasteur treatment." She was obviously referring to the Pasteur remedy for rabies, a malady I might have feared had I been bitten by a dog.

There was only one thing to do. Call the vet first and then call my doctor.

Both the veterinarian and the medical doctor agreed. Immunization against tetanus is very important, especially for horses and horsemen. Tetanus is a bacteria which hates oxygen, likes dirt, and is thrilled about horse manure.

Tetanus is always around horses, says R. J. Brown, D.V.M., and it is a killer, so it's a good idea to have your horses immunized.

"Although tetanus is present with all wounds, it is much more common if the wound was made by a puncture," Dr. Brown says. "Tetanus bacteria likes to get away from oxygen, and does very well in a deep, contaminated puncture."

To protect your horse, you should start a toxoid program. This involves two injections of tetanus toxoid four to six weeks apart, and then a booster shot at 12-month intervals.

There is a lot of confusion among horsemen about tetanus toxoid and tetanus antitoxin, according to Wayne O. Kester, D.V.M. One is safe to use, the other less so.

Tetanus toxoid is safe, effective and long-lasting. The only adverse effect ever observed is an occasional and temporary swelling at the point of injection.

Tetanus antitoxin, on the other hand, often gives excellent protection for two or three weeks, but its use sometimes results in serious and possibly fatal aftereffects, he said. The problem with antitoxin is that it contains horse serum, and horse serum injections are too frequently followed by equine serum hepatitis, which can be fatal.

Why may a veterinarian be forced to use tetanus antitoxin in spite of its drawbacks? Because in the absence of records or knowledge that the horse is being protected by a current toxoid program, he must use the antitoxin because it gives immediate protection, whereas toxoid does not unless the horse is on a protective program.

Because of the risks of using antitoxin, it is wise to start your horse on a toxoid program and keep him on one.

The symptom of tetanus is muscle stiffening. The animal has a rigid posture with the head and tail extended. Usually the first muscles affected are those of the jaws, which accounts for the common name, lockjaw.

In humans, the incubation period of tetanus is two to 50 days, says Peter G. Van Etten, M.D. The most frequent symptom, of course, is a stiffness of muscles, especially those of the jaws.

Dr. Van Etten said I wouldn't get tetanus from the bite, but that the tetanus spore might be on my skin and thereby get into the wound.

"Tetanus is dangerous and there are still a number of deaths caused by tetanus, especially among the young and very old," he said.

Most people should probably be immunized about every 10 years, but a person who works around horses should be immunized every five years. If you do suffer a wound, it should be washed immediately and then treated, Dr. Van Etten added.

The tetanus shot doesn't hurt when you get the needle. It hurts the next day.

I took the shot in my arm because it's hard to sit on a horse when you've had a shot in your bottom.

Coggins Test Controversy

The Coggins test. If you don't know about it, you had better learn the facts. If you do know about it, choose a side.

The Coggins test is quickly becoming the subject of the most vocal controversy to hit the horse world in years. And sooner or later, you will have to take a stand. A lot of horsemen already have, and they are fighting!

Here's the problem. Horses which are apparently quite healthy are being sentenced to death because tests show they are positive carriers of Equine Infectious Anemia (EIA), a disease that attacks the red blood cells, breaking them down and causing severe anemia.

In a little more than two years, approximately 18,000 horses have been sentenced to death because they reacted positively to the Coggins test. Incidental to the killing of the horses is the cost of doing away with them, nearly $22 million, according to R. A. Greene, D.V.M., of Temple, N.H.

Was it necessary to kill 18,000 positive reactors?

Maybe not. Research work now under way would indicate positive reactors, or carriers, are not necessarily dangerous to themselves or to other horses. They are definitely not dangerous to man, as the disease is not transferrable to humans, according to Dr. Greene.

How many horses die from EIA?

The answer to that question is at the center of the argument.

Apparently just how accurate anyone's figures are is questionable. Man has killed more horses in the past two years trying to stop the disease than the disease has killed in the past 40 years.

Shocking? Yes. But don't pick a side yet. Let's examine the problem a little more closely.

EIA makes horses quite sick, but it is not always fatal. There isn't a sure cure for the disease, and many horses, even after blood transfusions, continue to suffer from the malady, reports Richard J. Brown, D.V.M., of Norco, Calif.

The disease can spread anywhere because many healthy horses are carriers, or positive reactors to tests, even though they don't show physical signs of EIA.

The disease is spread from infected horses to sound horses by blood-sucking insects, Dr. Brown says.

But maybe, in more cases, it is spread by men, using dirty needles to inject horses suffering from colds, coughs or infections. (This suspected method of passing on the disease is a good argument for the disposable syringe and needle and should be, for the good horseman, enough to get him fighting mad about the careless clod who pokes a horse with a little antibiotic in an unsterile needle, then resells him for a quick profit.)

With an understanding of how the disease is transferred, it is easy to see why concerned horsemen have been demanding a test for EIA, and why Dr. Leroy Coggin, a research scientist, came up with such a test.

The test is exposing a tremendous number (but a low percentage) of horses which have EIA, or at least react positively. In 1974, 354,412 horses were tested, and 9,059 were reactors.

Without a cure for EIA, the only way to eliminate any chance of a sick reactor horse being responsible for infecting another horse is to put down the sick horse. And that is what is being done.

There has been a demand for a requirement that all horses be tested for EIA before being shipped from one state to another, allowed to enter a major racetrack, or be entered in a public sale.

Twenty-nine states have adopted such a requirement. And now we are seeing the results of a major test program for EIA.

Until recently, there was no available data which would indicate just how widespread the disease is, or how many carriers there are. Only the tip of the iceberg was visible . . . those horses which were known to have died from EIA.

The whole iceberg is coming into vicw now. All thc horses which have the disease, and all those who carry it.

How can the disease be eliminated? As we are doing now?

Do we kill off several thousand horses to protect a million?

And, then, that final, stabbing question.

Have you had your horse tested?

If you do, and the horse is a positive reactor yet apparently healthy, will you have him put down?

Summer Salt Loss

As you sit around the pool sipping iced tea and catching a few rays to improve that summer tan, think of your horse and say, "salt."

The salt block you put in the manger last summer and the salt contained in the prepared grain mix you feed may not be sufficient.

As the temperature and humidity climb, you perspire and your horse sweats. It's the body's way of reducing heat buildup. The greater the sweat loss, the more need there is for salt and trace mineral replacement.

The average-sized horse needs 50 to 60 grams of salt each day. On a warm day, a horse may lose that much salt easily through sweating and urination. If he is worked moderately, he will lose even more.

To replace that amount of salt loss, the horse will have to have about a four-ounce intake of salt, according to the U.S. National Research Council. You'll have to make your own determination about how much salt your own horse needs by observing his behavior and condition.

Salt and trace minerals play an important role in keeping the horse healthy. And a big loss of salt through sweating can lead to a change in the horse's behavior and condition.

A horse which is deficient in salt and trace minerals usually shows it through physical and behavioral reactions. Chewing on fences and mangers and eating dirt are behavioral changes. Physical reactions can be a loss in weight, a rough coat and listless eyes. Also, the horse may show fatigue when he is being worked.

Significant loss of electrolytes (salts dissolved in body fluids) can also lead to excessive fatigue, muscle spasms and cramps, dehydration and exhaustion. These conditions are normally seen in the horse during stress situations, but they can also occur from moderate work in very hot weather.

The amount of salt contained in hay and grain may be fine during the winter months, but it may not be sufficient for the horse during the summer.

Since most prepared grain mixes list salt and trace minerals as ingredients, but don't tell you how much, you can't rely on them to provide enough salt.

Therefore, it's to the horse's benefit if you have salt constantly available in loose salt form. Loose salt is easier for a horse to eat than block salt. Unlike the cow, the horse's tongue is smooth, and he can't get enough salt just by licking a block.

When a horse is in desperate need of salt, he will sometimes chew off big hunks from a salt block or consume the whole thing. Salt in this large an amount can cause a colic condition.

Horses don't like the red salt block, which is iodized salt, as well as they do the white block of salt.

Do not give a horse salt once a week, a practice which is fairly common, but incorrect. A horse cannot store salt in his system, so he'll be oversupplied one day, short the next.

Salt serves the horse in a number of ways. It stimulates the secretion of saliva, making food more palatable and aiding digestion. As a nutrient, it provides sodium and chlorine, which are necessary to establish and maintain the correct electrolytic balance.

A horse which is getting enough salt each day enjoys better health and has greater endurance.

Another summer problem related to salt and sweating is the condition of the horse's coat.

The hairs fade in color and dry out during the summer months. We sometimes say the horse's coat is sun-bleached and think there is little we can do about it.

It's my opinion, however, that the sun bleaching or coat fading is actually the result of damaged hair shafts and pigment patterns which no longer reflect light normally. The hair shafts are damaged or cracked by sweat drying on them.

If you will give your horse a cool, clear water rinse daily, you'll be washing away this saline solution, and in doing so, will be protecting the hair shaft from damage. The best time for rinsing him off each day is shortly after the hottest part of the afternoon.

Keeping a horse out of the sun altogether won't save his coat in the summer. If it's warm, he'll sweat, even if you don't notice much dampness.

Instead of keeping the horse locked in a dark stall, try the clear water bath. It's better for him in two ways. First, he needs to be in the sunshine, and second, his coat will stay nicer.

And do nice things for your horse. He's the salt of the earth.

Floating And Teeth

Horses sometimes need an orthodontist, and they always need an annual checkup by the horse dentist.

Horses have a lot of teeth. Some they lose, some are capped, some need floating, some tell their age and some make nice jewelry.

The mature horse has 40 teeth, while the mare has 36, usually. The stallion or gelding has "tushes," or pointed teeth between the incisors and molars. Tushes are not usually found in mares.

Sometimes horses and mares will develop small,

pointed teeth in front of the molars of the upper jaw. These teeth are known as "wolf" teeth.

Wolf teeth do not often appear in the lower jaw, but they can.

If a horse has all his teeth, plus wolf teeth, he could have as many as 44 teeth, while a mature mare could have as many as 40.

The horse which needs an orthodontist is in big trouble. It's not so much that his teeth are crooked as it is that they don't meet properly. This is the case of the parrot-mouthed horse whose upper teeth stick out in front of the lower teeth. Little can be done to help the parrot-mouthed horse, since the problem is more with the jaw than the teeth.

The horse which has mismatched teeth cannot chew its food well and therefore generally exhibits poor condition. Parrot-mouth is considered a genetic defect and parrot-mouthed horses should not be bred.

The horse dentist is usually your local veterinarian, and he should check the horse's teeth for general health and to see if they need floating.

Floating is really the rasping of rough, sharp edges. The rasp used to do the job is called a float.

Since the horse's upper jaw is wider than the lower jaw, the outside edge of the upper molars and the inside edge of the lower molars are not worn smooth during the grinding process of chewing. These sharp edges can cut the inside of the horse's mouth, and, consequently, need to be rasped smooth so the horse can chew properly again and feel comfortable.

Caps are really the young horse's baby molars. As the permanent molars come in, the baby molars often sit on top of the new teeth like a cap. These caps eventually fall off and end up in the manger.

And since the horse doesn't believe in the tooth fairy, you can have the caps. They make very nice jewelry. Polished, the caps are a creamy ivory color, streaked with dark brown swirls. In a pretty setting, the caps make interesting rings, tie tacks and pendants.

The six lower incisors reveal the horse's age – up to a point.

A foal gets his two middle nippers at 2 weeks of age. He'll have all six at about 8 months.

There are grooves in these incisors. The grooves disappear in the middle two teeth at 1 year, from the second pair at 2, and from the corner teeth at 3.

Starting with the middle two, these incisors are lost at age 2, 3 and 4. At 5, the horse has a whole new set, and each has a dark spot in the middle.

Again, starting with the center two, this spot disappears at 6, 7 and 8. When these cups have disappeared, we call the horse "smooth," meaning he is 9 or older. The cups disappear on the upper incisors at 9, 10 and 11 years of age. After that, it's hard to tell the horse's age.

The teeth, however, don't get shorter with age. Instead, they get longer, become triangular instead of round, and have a greater forward angle.

Looking in a horse's mouth is important, for the horse's health and your peace of mind.

But never look a gift horse in the mouth. You're not supposed to know his age.

Those Annoying Splints

Someone must come to the defense of the splint. I guess I'm the one.

I am fearful that many a good horse has been ignored or looked upon in disgrace due to the obvious, but most often harmless, splint.

In general terms, splints are bony enlargements located most frequently on the inside of the front cannon bones, which run from the hock joint to the fetlock and support the leg.

In more technical terms, splints can be caused by one or more of three different types of problems – a fracture of the splint bone, an inflammation of the binding ligament or an inflammation on the splint or cannon bone.

Small in size now, the splint bones are the remnants of toes lost long ago during the course of evolution. They are located just below the horse's knees on both the outside and inside of the cannon bone.

Today, the splint bones serve no purpose. They are simply tiny bones with little movement which are attached to the cannon by ligaments. The splint bone rests innocently waiting for evolution to eliminate it entirely when suddenly it is subjected to violent jarring, concussion or twisting.

Pow! The splint bone fractures and swelling occurs. The body's normal reaction in repairing fractures is to develop new bones which unite the two pieces of bone. Hence, a lump appears.

Or, the swelling may appear because the ligament which binds the splint bone to the cannon bone has been torn or stretched, or the outer lining of one or both of the bones has been damaged.

The swelling is painful, but seldom causes the horse to become seriously lame.

At the first sign of lameness or painful swelling, the horse must be rested. In the case of a fracture, a rest period of about six weeks is recommended. In the case of ligament or bone lining damage, the rest period should be longer — up to 10 weeks.

I like to run cool water on the injured area twice a day for about 20 or 30 minutes. A supportive bandage often helps.

In the case of a fracture, some veterinarians recommend surgical removal of part of the bone. Blistering and firing may be recommended if no fracture is present. But I don't like either method of treatment, as often the treatment is more dangerous than the problem.

If the injury is caught early, the period of rest, the water treatment to reduce heat and swelling and a supportive bandage will usually do the trick.

The owner's main concern should be that the injury is not aggravated by continued strain or concussion. Lameness can become serious, even permanent, if the enlargement should press into the suspensory ligament or tendons which run down the back of the horse's leg.

Splints most often occur when a young horse is asked to perform exercises of which he is not yet capable. Too often the novice horseman disregards good suppling and conditioning exercises and moves ahead with fast and punishing work.

Splints can occur naturally when young horses play too rough, or they can happen when the horse's conformation is such that the left or right cannon bone is struck by the opposite foot during movement.

While many judges of halter classes mark a horse down because of splints, I don't, unless their cause is obviously the result of poor conformation which causes one foot to strike the opposite cannon. If the horse travels straight, but has splints, I write the problem off to the unfortunate circumstance that the horse's evolutionary process is not yet complete.

Once healed, splints usually never bother the horse again.

So splints, while obvious blemishes in symmetry, are not usually as bad as their reputation.

On The Hoof

Everywhere I look, I see the foundation of the horse being undermined, neglected and mistreated.

Horses are staggering about aimlessly, their feet flopping in every direction.

I ask, "Upon what will the future of the horse stand if not upon the hoof?"

And the answer I get is, "I was going to take care of his feet last week, but I forgot."

"No foot, no horse." The saying is truer today than ever before.

We're breeding horses with feet too small for their size and weight.

We worry about the horse's coat, but seldom expend any effort on the hoof. And when we do, it's often a dab of hoof polish to cover past sins. And we shoe too early, often for the wrong reasons, and most of the time, improperly.

Worst of all, because it is the cause of the other problems, is the fact that the average horse owner doesn't understand the structure of the horse's hoof.

The exterior parts of the hoof include the wall, the sole, the bars, the heel and the frog. The normal, healthy foot is strong, smooth and well-balanced. Front feet are larger, rounder and stronger than hind feet since they carry more of the horse's total weight. The shape of the hind feet is best suited to the function of driving the horse.

Any ridges, rings, cracks in the hoof, or an unbalanced shape, should be considered unhealthy and abnormal.

The wall, or exterior surface of the hoof, is hard. It covers the highly sensitive interior parts of the foot and protects them from injury. These parts include the bones, laminae, plantar cushion, various tendons and ligaments, blood vessels and nerves. The wall has the greatest ground contact and supports most of the horse's weight.

The wall grows down continually from the coronary band, and excess growth must be removed. The healthy hoof grows three-eighths to one-half inch per month and should be trimmed every 30 days.

Shoeing is not necessary for the average pleasure horse unless the horse will be traveling frequently on severe terrain.

The sole of the foot is a concave, fairly soft, shelly growth. The sole and the frog of the feet do not grow indefinitely, but naturally discard excessive flakes or scales once they reach the natural thickness required to protect the healthy hoof from injury. The sole and the frog should never be cut away. Only dead flakes or ragged edges should be removed.

The bars of the foot are actually extensions of the wall, acting as a brace to keep the foot from over expansion as weight is placed upon it.

The heel is quite sensitive and has only the protection of a thin wall. It should be checked constantly because it is subject to painful ground burns or bruises.

The frog is the "V" shaped elastic substance with the wide base at the heel and the apex at the center of the hoof.

The frog has several functions. It absorbs the shock of weight, allows for expansion and contractions of the hoof, provides moisture to the entire hoof, and acts as a pump, forcing blood in and out of the foot.

To do its work properly, the frog must touch the ground, and should not be pared lower than the wall.

Inside the healthy and properly shaped hoof, the major bones and ligaments are adjusted and balanced in such a way that there are no unequal strains. Everything is in harmony, until something gets out of balance through lack of care, or improper care.

Trimming or shoeing, whether corrective or otherwise, should only be done to protect, preserve or restore the natural angle, health and balance of the hoof.

Horseshoes are unnatural, but when used, should be applied in the size, thickness and weight which interferes the least with the natural design of the hoof while doing the most to assist the horse in performing his best.

Here are some good rules to stand on.

Shoe only to protect the hoof, maintain good balance, or correct an unnatural flight of the foot.

Never allow a hoof to be rasped to fit a shoe. The shoe must be made to fit the foot.

Check and clean the horse's feet daily.

Don't use hoof polish or conditioners with unnatural ingredients.

In dry areas, apply natural conditioners frequently enough to maintain hoof flexibility and elasticity.

Make sure the hoof gets plenty of moisture.

And finally ... don't put your toe under a healthy hoof!

CHAPTER VI

Historical Hoofnotes

I cannot tell a lie. George Washington's famous war horse, Nelson, was not white, as he was so often depicted by painters. He was a light chestnut.

Little is known about Washington's horses, other than Nelson and a prized racehorse, Magnolio, as Washington spelled it.

There is evidence Washington was mounted on a white horse during the Battle of Trenton in 1777. The horse had been a gift from the Continental governor of New Jersey.

It was reported that during the battle, which went on for quite some time, Washington spared neither himself nor his horse, and that the horse became so exhausted he died of fatigue.

But Nelson, a gift from Gov. Thomas Nelson Jr. of Virginia, apparently seemed never to tire. He carried Washington, who weighed about 200 pounds, through many of the battles of the Revolutionary War. He endured the miserable winter at Valley Forge and was there to accept the surrender of Lord Cornwallis after the Battle of Yorktown in 1781.

Nelson was a big-boned gelding and came into Washington's possession at the age of 3. Washington loved to fox hunt and for 10 years prior to the outbreak of armed conflict, Nelson was his favorite hunter.

When Washington was named commander in chief of the rebel force, he rode Nelson from Philadelphia to Boston, where he assumed command of his troops.

Since Nelson was Washington's first choice as a mount, it is safe to assume the horse was strong, a good mover, an excellent jumper, had good endurance and a calm disposition. Washington was a skilled horseman who would not have tolerated an inferior horse.

As well as Nelson served his master, it cannot be truthfully said he was Washington's favorite horse. The title of favorite goes to Magnolio, an Arabian sired by Ranger.

Magnolio was at the top of the list of Washington's inventory of stock recorded in 1785, just two years before he was to become the first President of the United States.

Magnolio stood at stud at Mount Vernon through the breeding seasons of 1785 and 1788.

Washington was quite successful with most things he attempted, but it was Magnolio which taught him you can't win them all.

In the only recorded match race between horses owned by a President of the United States and a future President, Magnolio lost to a roan colt owned by Thomas Jefferson. The race was held at the Jockey Club in Alexandria, Va., and it was reported that Magnolio was "badly beaten."

Magnolio was sold, or in truth, traded by Washington to Light Horse Harry Lee for 5,000 acres of land in Kentucky.

With Magnolio went Washington's dream of becoming the foremost breeder of fine racehorses, so Washington took up a new pursuit — he became the first famous colonist to breed mules.

Washington's first "jackass of the best breed" was a gift from the king of Spain and was named Royal Gift. He was, however, a sluggish and poor breeder.

Not wanting to be outdone by Spain, the Marquis de Lafayette of France sent Washington a jack and two jennetts. The jack was named Knight of Malta and proved to be a good breeder but had a bad disposition.

From these two lines, Washington got a jack which he called Compound, which had the size of Royal Gift and the courage of Knight of Malta. Compound had a significant effect on mule raising in the United States, a venture which proved most successful for Washington.

The Midnight Goof Of Paul Revere

Contrary to the belief made popular by poet Henry Wadsworth Longfellow, Paul Revere blew it.

His supposedly wild gallop from Boston to Concord to warn, "The British are coming," was really a slow stroll into a trap, which led to his capture by the British, which led to his failure to warn the minutemen of Concord, which led to the loss of his horse, which didn't even belong to him.

Yes, April 16, 1775, was just one of those nights when everything went wrong for Paul.

He finally recorded the actual story on his 63rd birthday, 23 years after the ride.

According to Revere, things happened this way.

It was learned the British planned to seize the arms cache at Concord and capture Samuel Adams and John Hancock, who were in Lexington, Mass. Dr. John Warren, head of the Committee of Safety, learned of the British plan, and devised one of his own.

Warren sent a committee member, Sam Dawes, to Lexington to warn Adams and Hancock. When two lights appeared in the church belfry, Revere knew the British were crossing the Charles River, and he started his ride to Lexington.

Revere was riding a mare, loaned to him by Deacon Larkin, a friend.

The mare was a chestnut Narragansett Pacer, described by Revere as a "very good horse." Her name never was revealed.

The Narragansett Pacer was unquestionably the most popular saddle horse in America at the time. Bred in Rhode Island in lush pastures bounded by the Atlantic Ocean and the Narragansett Bay, the horses were on the small side, had good dispositions, great endurance, good manners and an ambling gait.

Their gait made them very pleasant to ride, even though the gait was not always a pace, in which both legs of the same side move at the same time.

This hearty little horse was much in demand by Caribbean planters who supervised the labor of the sugarcane fields, and thereby became a major economic influence on Rhode Island life.

By the time of the Civil War, however, the breed was virtually extinct, a victim of mechanization and population growth.

As Revere rode along at an ambling pace, he was spotted by two British soldiers, who immediately pursued him. Revere escaped when one of the British soldiers rode his horse into a pond and his companion stopped to help.

Revere arrived in Lexington in time to warn Adams and Hancock. Then he met Sam Dawes and they decided to rest their horses before going on to Concord. The whole trip was only 16 miles, hardly a warm-up for a good Narragansett Pacer.

Apparently Paul and Sam were not impressed by the urgency of the matter, for up to this time, they had been averaging about five miles an hour. A horse normally walks four miles an hour.

Fortunately for the American Revolution, Paul and

Sam met Dr. Samuel Prescott, who was on his way home to Concord.

The doctor was courting a young lady, not making a house-on-horse call.

As they rode along, Dawes left the road to warn the occupants of a farmhouse. While Dawes was gone, four British soldiers captured Prescott and Revere.

Prescott saw an opportunity to escape, put the spurs to his horse, raced across a pasture, jumped a stone wall, and was off into the night. Revere tried to take advantage of the confusion, and rode off in the other direction, head-on into six more British soldiers. He was recaptured.

Dawes, alerted by the sound of the soldiers, took off at a gallop for Concord, but fell from his horse and also was captured.

Revere and the six soldiers started back for Lexington. But after about a mile, the commanding officer, Maj. Mitchell, ordered Paul to give his horse to a sergeant whose horse was tired. Paul did so. He was left to walk home.

The British soldiers rode on to Lexington in time to retreat with their fellow redcoats.

What happened to the Narragansett Pacer Revere rode is not known.

However, it is a good bet Prescott also was riding a Narragansett Pacer, and he did reach Concord, spreading the word of the British advance and alerting the minutemen for the shot heard 'round the world.

Black Jack Was The Last

Black Jack is dead. And with his death, an era has passed into history.

Black Jack was the last horse to be branded with the Army's "U.S." brand. He was the last of the quartermaster-issued horses. There will be no more.

The victim of old age, Black Jack celebrated his

29th birthday on Jan. 28, 1976. It was a regal ceremony for unquestionably the most famous of the riderless horses which follow behind the funeral caissons of Presidents, high ranking military officers and fallen warriors.

Black Jack was the caparisoned (riderless) horse which touched the hearts of the millions who saw the televised funeral of President John F. Kennedy. He also followed behind the funeral caisson of Presidents Lyndon B. Johnson and Herbert Hoover and General of the Army Douglas MacArthur. He served in the 3rd U.S. Infantry at Fort Myer, Va., for 24 years.

The practice of having the horse of a deceased military officer led in the funeral procession survives an ancient custom of sacrificing a horse at the burial of a warrior.

In the days of Genghis Khan, the Mongols and Tartars believed the spirit of the sacrificed horse would follow to serve its master's spirit in the afterworld.

As late as 1781, when General Kasimer was buried at Treves, his horse was killed and placed in the grave with the dead general. According to the European folk belief, the general's spirit would have had to walk had it not had a spirit mount.

Blackbird, an Omaha chief, was buried sitting on his favorite mount sometime around 1800. This was the custom adopted by some American Plains Indians.

President Abraham Lincoln was the first U.S. President honored by the inclusion of the caparisoned horse in his funeral cortege. Lincoln's own horse was used in the funeral, as were the President's boots, which were, by tradition, placed backwards in the saddle.

When a caparisoned horse is completely black, as was Black Jack, then the only tack it carries is the saddle blanket, saddle and bridle. However, if the horse is of any other color, a full hood and cape must be worn by the animal.

The cape buttons at the chest in front of the left leg. It has a crupper which fits under the horse's tail to hold the cape in place. The cape hangs to the hocks and knees, and is bordered by three-inch long fringe and six-inch long tassels spaced every four inches.

The hood covers the head and neck to the withers. It buttons under the jaw and down the neck to the chest. The hood has eye slots and extends to the edge of the mouth. The horse's ears are completely covered by fringed ear pieces.

An English saddle is used on the caparisoned horse, and the boots, with spurs, are placed backwards in the stirrups, then fastened at the top to the stirrup leathers. On the off-side, an officer's field saber and carrier is placed. The carrier is fastened to the saddle. At the bottom of the carrier, a strap runs under the horse and fastens to the cantle on the near side. This keeps the saber in a vertical position.

The riderless horse follows the caisson, a horse-drawn artillery ammunition wagon or carriage, upon which rides the flag-draped casket of the fallen warrior.

Today there are 30 mounts in the Caisson Platoon, the only active U.S. Army unit authorized to have horses. The horses are used primarily for full-honor funerals at Arlington National Cemetery overlooking the Potomac River in Washington, D.C.

A matched team of six horses pulls the caisson. Normally six grays pull the caisson for a week, then six blacks work for a week.

The wheel pair – the heaviest and closest to the caisson – is led by a swing pair, with the lead pair in front. Although all six horses are saddled, only the near side horses are mounted. One rider to a pair is a custom which began in the days of the horse-drawn artillery, when one horse of the pair carried provisions.

A fourth rider, the section sergeant in charge of the detail, precedes the caisson. He rides an unhitched horse.

Most of the horses in today's unit are about 15 hands. All are light draft geldings, and most come from Virginia, Oklahoma or Texas.

One exception is Conversano Be'ja, a famous Lipizzaner stallion presented to the Army by the Austrian government in 1964. Conversano, being white, serves as the section sergeant's horse only when the gray team is used.

The active duty time of the horses varies, but when one is too old to serve, he is retired to pasture at Fort Meade, Md.

Black Jack had been retired since 1973.

His funeral was conducted in the tradition reserved for high-ranking officers.

The Four Horsemen

Here are some revelations about the four horsemen of the Apocalypse. Actually, there were five. Most people think they know who they were, but don't. And it's darn hard to find out much about them.

It would seem that horsemen could easily recall the four horsemen. They were conjured up in the visions of John, author of the Book of Revelation. He does not claim to be John the Apostle, although he has been so identified by early fathers of the Catholic Church.

When asked, it is not unusual for a horseman to name famine and death. But it is rare to find a person who can name three. Usually, the third horseman most often named is pestilence, which has to do with infectious disease leading to death, and is not correct.

Actually, the four horsemen of the Apocalypse are: 1. the rider of the white horse, the conquerer; 2. the rider of the red horse, war; 3. the rider of the black horse, famine; 4. the rider of the sickly green horse, death.

Apocalypse means revelation, discovery, disclosure,

and is normally applied to the Book of Revelation, the last book of the New Testament.

The Book of Revelation is an account of John's visions, written in symbolic and allegorical language. He wrote in a symbolic manner because the Book of Revelation was resistance literature, written in a time of crisis. It was most likely written during the reign of the Roman Domitian (81-96 A.D.), who was a fierce persecutor of the Christians.

John's visions were foretelling the destiny of the world. Because he was speaking of the world, he used the code number of four, which at the time signified the world. The horsemen, therefore, were to have a significant effect on the world.

The first horseman rode a white horse, symbolic of the Parthians on the eastern border of the Roman empire. The rider of the white horse carried a bow, again a reference to the Parthians, whose army of mounted bowmen were dreaded. The Parthians won a great battle against the Romans in 62 A.D., and for Christians of the time, this was a joyous event. This victory may be part of the reason the rider was mounted on a white horse and given a crown, which symbolized victory.

Throughout later history, great generals were most often pictured on white horses, whether or not they owned one.

The second rider rode a red horse and was given a sword, the symbol for war. The rider was given the power to rob the world of peace by allowing men to kill one another. The sword could also have meant civil war, not among Christians, but among Jews. The Jewish rebellion was a civil war and ended with the sacking of Jerusalem in 70 A.D.

The third rider rode a black horse and carried a pair of scales. The black horse symbolized famine, a normal occurrence in ancient times following a war.

The fourth rider rode a sickly green horse, the symbol of death. In the long robe which trailed behind him were all of the nether world, presumably all of the dead who were buried below the earth's surface.

The green horse is also considered at times to represent the other three horses and all the woes of the world to follow. Persons might be expected to avoid the conqueror, or war, or famine, but never all three.

The fifth rider mentioned in the Book of Revelation also rode a white horse, and we must assume he was Christ, for his name was written on a "cloak that covered his thigh: 'King of Kings and Lord of Lords'."

The fifth rider, according to the author, had justice as his standard – and the armies of heaven, also on white horses, rode behind him. They wore fine linen, pure and white. The description of the fifth rider is carried in the 19th chapter, where John tells of the destruction of the pagan nations.

The four horsemen of the Apocalypse rode for another author, Vincente Blasco Ibanez. His four horsemen were also visions, as his work was fiction. He wrote well, but the book was not particularly popular, although a motion picture was later made from it.

The four horsemen of the Apocalypse still ride, even if we can't always name them in order. They still affect our lives and maybe always will.

Tall In The Saddle

As far as I know, he was one of the few Presidents who never had his picture taken on a horse.

He might have, though. He was a natural horseman and had learned to ride at about the same time he learned to walk.

Maybe it never occurred to anyone at the time. Or maybe the photographers thought he'd appear too gaunt, too tall to look like a cavalier on horseback. (Someone should have had similar thoughts about President Jimmy Carter, who was photographed on an

Appaloosa for publicity purposes. I may be the only one to say it, but President Carter did not look like a horseman. I guess someone else thought as I did, for the photograph later became a painting, with a few corrections, and was presented to the Appaloosa Horse Club, Inc. I don't know what happened to the original photo.)

Our unmounted President actually owned four horses, all of which were purchased for utilitarian reasons.

His first horse was what some might call a "nag." It was acquired at a cost of $50. The young, freelance surveyor used the horse in his work, but not for long. Shortly after he bought the horse, it was taken from him as part of a judgment secured against an old debt. The horse was sold at a public auction, along with the young man's equipment, but it was bought by a friend, who returned it to our hero after he agreed to repay the friend.

A few months later, the young man rode his $50 horse 75 miles to the state legislature at Vandalia, but he didn't ride him home. The horse was stolen.

That horse was the second of three he lost to horse thieves. When he was a newly elected captain of the New Salem volunteers, he rode a horse which had been loaned to him by a neighbor. The horse was stolen after the outfit was mustered out of service at Black Water, Wis., and the young man had to walk home, a distance of nearly 100 miles.

He lost another horse, which also had been loaned to him, in March of 1836. An advertisement in the Springfield newspapers requested return of the horse which either "strayed" or was "stolen."

Bad luck with horses didn't stop the six-foot, four-inch newly named lawyer. He bought a horse named Buck to ride the circuit of Springfield County, Ill., and for the next 14 years, he hitched Buck to a buggy, and as they drove along, he contemplated the problems which confronted the country. When the roads were too muddy for a carriage, he would ride the horse.

Buck eventually got too old to travel the circuit and was replaced by a horse named Tom. Tom cost the goodly sum of $125, and was supposed to be a sound, all-purpose horse. Whether or not he was is questionable, because it was not long before Tom was replaced by Bob or Robin, both names being applied to the horse the owner had when he was elected President of his country.

It was the law at the time that the government paid for the groom, driver, and upkeep of White House horses. The horses had to be provided by the President, and what horses this President provided, I don't know, for Robin was sold just before the new President moved into the White House.

Two of the President's sons had ponies during the time they lived at the White House. Both ponies were destroyed, however, when the White House stables burned on the night of Feb. 10, 1864.

On several occasions, the President rode horseback when he inspected the troops of the Union Army, and at one time, he rode the favorite mount of General Grant, a bay gelding known as Cincinnati. On previous other rides, the President's mount was a cavalry horse appropriately named Old Abe.

But it was Robin, the horse he sold before moving into the White House, which returned, and draped in black, walked behind the hearse which bore the assassinated Abraham Lincoln.

Racing Fever

Undefeated Triple Crown winner Seattle Slew quickly became defeated Slew.

Three times horse-of-the-year Forego got nipped by a nose.

That's horse racing.

But is anyone complaining? Nope.

Everyone is looking forward to another test, and another, and another, and another.

It's been that way with horses and racing for nearly 9,000 years. As far as we know, that's when chariot racing began, according to ancient writings and drawings. Maybe it was earlier.

Flat racing started about 6,000 years ago, and by the year 1500 B.C., kings had established elaborate racing stables in Asia Minor.

The first formal mounted horse race was recorded at the 33rd Olympiad, held in Greece in 624 B.C. And organized racing as we know it originated in England in 1174 A.D. and Charles II (1660-85) was given the title of Father of the British Turf.

It is generally accepted that the first racetrack in America was founded in 1665 in New York by the then English governor, Col. Richard Nicolls, to promote the improvement of American horses. The race course was called the Newmarket Course and was on the Hempstead Plain, Long Island, near the site of the present Belmont Park.

All U.S. racehorses can be traced back to the Byerly Turk, the Godolphin Barb and the Darley Arabian because in 1793, there were only three Thoroughbreds in the Stud Book which perpetuated themselves. And those three were descendants of the Turk, the Barb and the Arabian.

Today, a good Thoroughbred runs at speeds of 38 to 40 miles an hour, and fans wager somewhere close to $50 billion a year on their noses.

The average bettor goes to the $2 window and spends only $4 a day. It's interesting that the $2 ticket still costs $2 and has since pre-depression days. Everything else about horse racing has gone up and up and up, including the price of the "tip" sheet.

About 75 million persons make wagers on horse

racing in the United States each year, but only a small percentage of them are professional gamblers. According to track surveys, of the men who wager, 50 per cent are businessmen, professors, judges and politicians. Of the women, 88 per cent are housewives.

Match racing has long been popular in America.

Here are some facts about match racing which should help you determine the winner.

Match races have always been won by the horse which has the most early speed on that particular day. In most cases, the winner leads wire to wire, or the winning horse opens a long lead and maintains it. The winner has never come from behind.

CHAPTER VII

Working Horses

Endurance Racing Takes Off

If you think you're a good rider . . . if you think you've got a tough, fast horse, try endurance racing. My guess is you'll be thinking twice!

I tried the Flying H Green Back Special, a 50-mile test of man and horse across terrain I didn't believe anyone would race over. The top 10 riders ran at full speed down rocky washes, across meadows, along mountain ridges, down steep slopes, and when they came to hills too steep for a horse to gallop up, they jumped off their mounts, grabbed the horse's tail, and sent them up while they dragged along behind.

The first 11 miles of the race were run at an average speed of better than 22 miles an hour. Kathie Perry, super star of endurance racing, won the event in a little more than four hours at an average speed of better than 12 miles an hour for the 50 miles.

I rode a horse named Winston. Winston is owned by California Thoroughbred trainer Jerry Fanning of Arcadia. I completed 36 miles of the race in just a little more than an hour longer than it took Kathie Perry to win it.

But I was happy. And so was Winston when we quit. Winston is a great horse, but he's a pony horse at the major California racetracks and just not ready for mountain climbing.

Endurance racing, as we know it today, started about 22 years ago with the first running of the Western States Pony Express 100-mile, one-day ride. The ride, now known as the Tevis Cup, originated to prove or disprove the argument that today's horses are as strong as horses were 100 years ago.

There's little doubt in my mind that today's horses are just as tough, and consistent endurance race competitors are tougher.

Five years ago, there were about a dozen races in the United States. Today, there are more than 100 rides each year and the sport is growing rapidly.

In endurance racing, every precaution is taken to protect the horses. Little concern is given to the riders with the exception of young competitors, who must be accompanied by an adult sponsor.

There is usually one veterinarian in attendance for each 20 horses. And passing vet checks, which are set up about every 10 miles, isn't easy. Your horse must be in great condition and you have to know how to keep him that way, even under the terrible stress of the race.

To be a good endurance rider, you need a sound horse. You must ride many, many miles each week to train him, and you must have a complete understanding of heart rates, respiration, hydration, muscle composition and leg structure. And you need to develop a sixth sense which tells you how much more your horse can take. And you need experience.

Just how hard a ride was the Green Back Special? Well, some riders who had been on the 100-mile Tevis Cup told me the Tevis Cup was a warmup for the Green Back Special.

Pepper High Hand, an Appaloosa ridden by Jack Garnett, who had scored enough victories to be fifth in the year-end high point endurance ride awards for California, tied up and went into convulsions and was almost lost during the Green Back Special.

And out of 69 starters, only 42 finished. Among those who didn't make the 50 miles was Pathfinder, a famous endurance horse which had won more than $6,000 the previous year.

It's tough. But the challenge and the totally objective results are what makes endurance racing grow. And the sport is growing so fast that now there is the Endurance Horse Registry of America. Horses to be registered can be of any breed, but must compete and score high in a specified number of races which have a minimum number of contestants.

Arabians will dominate endurance riding for the next few years simply because there are so many Arabians involved in the sport. However, it is my guess they will dominate forever because the Arabian is physically better-suited to such an event than other breeds. The Arabian has an undeniable better recovery rate and can, because of its conformation, take in oxygen more quickly than can other breeds.

Saddle Gymnastics

I predict vaulting will be a very big sport in America.

The art of gymnastics on a moving horse, vaulting is extremely popular in Europe, growing in America, and under consideration as a contest to be included in the Olympic games.

Add the fact that lots of pretty, young girls are becoming vaulters, and the sport can't miss.

One such lady is Debby Haueter of Chino, Calif. A student at California Polytechnic Institute in Pomona, Debby is apparently minoring in agribusiness management. From her enthusiasm, it appears her major is vaulting.

Debby began vaulting a year ago and in the first few months attained a skill level rated 'bronze.'

Vaulters are awarded levels – bronze, silver and gold – by competing in sanctioned American Vaulting Association (AVA) events.

Bronze-level vaulters, says Debby, may work on a horse which is moving at either the trot or canter, while silver and gold level vaulters must work on a horse which is cantering.

Jeannine Vore, vaulting and equitation instructor at California Polytechnic, says vaulting had its beginning when the Romans were masters of the world. It was a means of training soldiers to ride. During the Middle Ages, knights practiced vaulting as a practical way of improving their balance and timing.

"Of course, today we do more intricate exercises," says Debby, "and we are most concerned with form and execution.

"And in the process, vaulters gain better body control, more rhythm and timing, greater balance and suppleness, and more courage and determination."

Courage and determination, yes! It takes both to run alongside a cantering horse, leap upon its back, do a semi-handstand, swing your body around so you are facing the horse's rear end, then dismount with a flip.

Naturally, you are wondering what kind of horse it takes to put up with nine or 10 gymnasts leaping on and off.

"Most any horse with a kind disposition works just fine," says Debby.

The real key to having a good vaulting horse – as with all other activities involving horses – is the initial training.

The vaulting horse must be taught to work on a longe line upon voice command. A steady, smooth gait is the goal sought. Once the horse has learned to maintain a steady pace, the rest is easy.

But even with that encouragement, don't run to the backyard and begin vaulting.

First, you need vaulting equipment, which amounts to a surcingle with handles positioned on each side of the horse's withers.

And vaulters usually learn their exercises and drills on a practice barrel. By using the barrel, the beginning vaulter learns the exercises required for competition at the very steady gait of a standstill. Also, the horse doesn't get overly tired while the beginner plays catch-up.

There are six basic exercises for vaulters. They are the riding seat, the flag, the mill, the stand, the scissors and the flank (dismount).

At higher levels, vaulters perform "kurs," which are free style exercises. Judging is based on skill and form.

As for me, I'm still trying to straddle that impossible barrel.

If You're Rich, Try Polo

If I were among the idle rich, I'd idle for awhile, and play polo the rest of the day.

Horsemen's heaven most certainly must have room for a polo field which, incidentally, is 300 yards long and 160 yards wide.

But in order to be in horsemen's heaven here on earth, you must be rich, idle, a skillful horseman, courageous and the owner of several good ponies of the polo variety.

No one knows where polo originated, but the game was played as long ago as 600 B.C. in Persia, Tibet, India and China.

The game was introduced in England about 1860, and the first match, billed as hockey on horseback, was played in 1869.

The English word, polo, comes from the Tibetan word, pulu, which means willow. Balls and mallets were originally made of willow wood.

The game is played with two teams, each with four members, a forward, a pivot man, a goal defender and a rover. The idea is to drive a compressed bamboo root or willow wood ball (3.5 inches in diameter, weighing four to 4.5 ounces and costing $150 a gross) through the opponent's goal.

The ball is driven with a mallet, which has a 49- to 53-inch handle and a rounded, wooden cross bar on the end. How well a player uses his mallet determines his rating, which is listed as zero to 10 goals.

The game is divided into six time periods called chukkers. Each chukker is seven and a half minutes long.

An extremely fast game — the horses are sometimes running at speeds up to 10 miles per hour — polo is also a punishing physical contest for both horse and rider.

It is permissible to ride off an opponent by bumping him with your horse as you both race for the ball. Horses fall, riders fall and broken bones are not uncommon. Riders and horses are frequently hit by the speeding ball, which can have the velocity of a baseball hit by Pete Rose.

So strenuous is the contest that most riders own and use two or three horses during a game.

Since most experts agree the pony contributes 70 to 75 per cent of the game, there has always been considerable interest in the breeding of good polo ponies.

Most of the early English breeders crossed small Thoroughbred sires with good foundation pony mares. Sir Humphrey de Tafford's Thoroughbred pony, Rosewater, is considered to be the foundation sire of the modern polo pony.

But breeding aside, the foremost criterion of a good polo pony is performance. First of all, he must have lots of heart and courage. He must be extremely fast from a standing start, and at a full gallop be able to stop quickly, pivot easily and have the temperament of a saint.

He must really know the game and love it, follow the ball on his own account, and place himself in relation to it so his rider is in the best position to strike the ball. Only one in 100 trained horses qualifies to play.

The polo pony is a type, rather than a breed.

The conformation of a good polo pony includes a long neck with narrow throatlatch, good sloping shoulders, a strong, short back and well-sprung ribs, a deep heart-girth, elbows well away from the body, powerful hindquarters and hocks well down. A fairly good polo pony costs about $7,000.

Tony Veen, general manager of the El Dorado Polo Club in Palm Desert, Calif., says it is best for the beginning polo player to start with an older, experienced pony and a stake of from $10,000 to $200,000 to get him through the season.

There are nine circuits in the United States and almost all games are played at private clubs. Polo is played all year long, players and their horses simply move from one private club to another as seasons change.

"There is no money in polo for the players or the professionals," says Veen. "It's simply a way of life."

Not to mention a good portion of your cash. But then, who considers that. It's the spirit that counts. Idle awhile, play awhile, idle awhile.

Ah, to be rated a 10-goal player!

Circus Stable

Mass confusion! Bands blare, clowns gesture, wild animals growl, pretty girls dance, elephants trumpet, and in the midst of it all, the liberty horses calmly go around and around in a complicated, intricate pattern.

A petite, blonde 14-year-old girl calls to the horses and up they go on their hind legs. Walking, then whirling, and then off at a gallop in the opposite direction. The motions of her hands change the checkerboard pattern of the four blacks and four grays again, and they swing into a new formation in the blur of a rhythmic lope.

What magic makes these horses work with complete freedom, yet with precision timing and control?

The magic of John Herriott, who modestly claims he's just starting to reach his potential, when in fact, he may already be the world's best circus horse trainer.

Herriott, whose father was also a trainer of circus horses, specializes in both the liberty horses and the high school horses. He is the performance director of the Ringling Brothers and Barnum & Bailey Circus, and has trained most of the horses which perform simultaneously in all three circus rings daily to the delight of thousands of spectators.

Herriott starts working on a liberty act by first selecting the horses by color.

"Remember, we're in the entertainment business, and the color and patterns of the horses are important to the visual impact of the show."

Herriott uses many breeds — Arabs, Morgans, Thoroughbreds, Andalusians and Appaloosas — but the Quarter Horse, he believes, makes one of the best liberty horses because of his ability to turn quickly and smoothly. It is one of Herriott's convictions, however, that a good trainer can get a good performance from almost any horse.

Once the horses are selected, Herriott begins training them. First, each horse must learn to stand on the picket line. Circus horses get plenty of bedding to lie on, but they never get a stall or corral.

"Each horse, whether stallion, mare, or gelding, must be taught to stand side-by-side without kicking or striking. They will spend lots of time on the picket line and we can't afford to have them hurt each other."

From the picket line, the horse goes to the longe line. They are worked on the line in the circus ring, which is 42 feet in diameter. They next learn the significance of the whip. Herriott's training calls for the whip to eventually replace the longe line, and actually, he says, the horse soon learns to think of the whip as a longe line and responds to it as if it were an attached line.

At this point in training, Herriott decides where each horse will fit into the act.

"I select the most aggressive horse as the lead horse, knowing the others will follow his lead. He is the key horse. The fifth horse must be the next most aggressive because when the group of eight is broken into separate patterns, he becomes the lead horse."

Once each horse is working at liberty as an individual, Herriott begins to work them in pairs. They are still on the longe line during each training session, but by now they're working without any restraint.

Herriott says that after several weeks of training, he can have a group of six horses working well enough to do a simple routine in a show. It takes up to a year to train larger groups of horses (up to 12 animals) to perform the more spectacular and complicated routines.

The question Herriott is asked most frequently is how does he keep a liberty horse in the ring.

"That's easy," he says with a friendly smile. "It's a matter of horse psychology. I have a few assistant trainers standing outside the ring. When a horse jumps out, they make a lot of noise and chase the horse around.

"When the horse finally comes back into the ring on his own, all the noise and chasing stops and the horse gets a reward of carrots.

"He soon learns that everything is good and peaceful in the circus ring, and that everything outside is mass confusion."

Fancy Talk For Basics

When you get down to the nitty-gritty, dressage may be a French word, but good trainers of western horses practice it every day.

So do the good trainers of English horses.

The style of saddle has nothing to do with it.

The fancy talk, high prices and snooty attitudes usually associated with dressage are, in my opinion, a coverup for the poor trainer who sells impressions instead of performance.

The good trainer sticks to basics, needs no facade and says it simply.

"Dressage is nothing more and nothing less than the dressing of the horse, meaning its conditioning, training and suppling, as you make it capable of doing the work you wish it to do," says Jennifer Vercoe of San Diego Country Estates in California.

Harrap's Standard French and English Dictionary offers the following: "Cheval au dressage. Horse in training, being broken in. Dressage training."

The dictionary may be the authority on the proper terminology, but Jennifer is an authority on performance. Her accomplishments are nothing short of outstanding.

Born and reared in Portugal of English parentage, she jumped as a representative of her country in the first Nation's Cup. In 1966, at the age of 19, she placed fifth in the Ladies European Jumping Championship.

She competed in the Ladies World Jumping Championship in Copenhagen in 1970, and for eight years, she competed in international horse shows of Olympic standard in Portugal, England, Germany, Switzerland, Spain, Morocco, Austria and Denmark.

She was preparing for the Munich Olympics when

love triumphed and she married. Today, she teaches advanced training techniques, side saddle and show jumping.

Dressage, she says, means basics. And basics are the most important element of horsemanship.

"You must gain the horse's respect. Not a fear of you, but respect for you. And you must develop the horse's muscles, suppling him to achieve both lateral and direct flexion.

"You should be able to extend and collect a horse on the longe line, and the horse must be able to respond perfectly on the longe before you ever ride."

Far too many trainers and riders skip lightly over the basics, Jennifer says, thinking they are good horsemen because they can get fast work from a horse. Their performance lacks form, beauty and grace.

It is the classical riders who have developed dressage (basic training techniques) into an art.

"For them, an exhibition of dressage is a series of predetermined intricate movements which express beauty, perfection and pleasure. There should be satisfaction for both the rider and spectator," Jennifer explains.

Competitive dressage involves a set pattern for exercises, and one rider competes against another.

"The best classical riders are from Spain, Portugal and Austria, while the best competitive riders are from Germany and Sweden."

Andalusian and Hanoverian horses make the best dressage horses, Jennifer claims. "It is simply because they are bred for that style of work. Thoroughbreds are good, too, but they have been bred for speed and dressage is done slowly and with finesse."

Jennifer is quick to point out that good western training techniques are quite similar to the dressage she speaks of. However, not as much time is spent training western horses, or for that matter, hunt horses.

"Many western horses and hunt horses exhibit skills, but no art," she says.

Jennifer claims it takes at least three years, possibly more, to train a good dressage horse.

"Most of the training is done on a snaffle bit. When we get a horse to the higher levels of performance, we use a low port curb."

Collection and impulsion are two principles which must be included in any discussion of dressage. Jennifer describes collection as starting with the horse's hindquarters, not the forehand.

"The horse is pushed onto the bit," she says. "Therefore, the hindquarters move the horse forward."

"Impulsion is that springiness you get with forward movement when the horse is using his muscles and is under control. You don't get impulsion from a lazy horse."

And that's dressage. Complete control and instant response to a series of cues which call for a particular performance.

It's something special, far beyond the normal, but not sacred and not reserved for the elite. It's available to every horseman.

The next time someone tries to put on airs and impress you with their boast, "I'm studying dressage," simply say, "How wonderful. I'm glad you're studying basic training methods. Are you going western or English?"

I think Jennifer Vercoe would like your comeback.

Barrel Racers Bring Most Money

What kind of horse is the highest-priced in rodeo?

Calf roping horse? Team roping horse? Bareback bronc?

None of the above.

The horse that brings the most money, time and time again, is the barrel racing horse.

"Paying more than $10,000 for a good barrel racer is not uncommon. And anything priced below $5,000 is suspect," says Lydia Moore, secretary-treasurer of the Girls Rodeo Association (GRA).

More than in any other rodeo contest, the horse and rider must be perfectly coordinated for barrel racing. Calf ropers and steer wrestlers often borrow someone else's mount. But not barrel racers.

"The slightest miscue, or a fraction of a second of hesitation by horse and rider, and you're out of the money," Lydia says.

Barrel racing is so exacting and the competition so keen that the price of a winning horse has gone up and up.

Good barrel horses must be extraordinary animals. They need spirit and sprint speed, which is why most of them are Quarter Horses. They also need the maneuverability of the polo pony.

A good barrel horse is solidly built, with great legs which can withstand the tremendous strain of sudden turns. He must be durable, both physically and mentally, as barrel horses are hauled many miles, endure frequent changes of climate, and have to adjust to differences in feed. The barrel racer must also accept and cope with the intense pressure of competition under constantly different circumstances.

A horse which can do all that has got to be worth plenty, Lydia says, especially to a girl who is winning several thousand dollars prize money each year.

And how much can a girl win in rodeo?

Well, Jimmie Gibbs won more than $20,000 last year. Connie Combs won more than $19,000, Gail Petska, more than $15,000, and Kay Vanvoras, more than $10,000.

But the average for the top 20 money winners in GRA last year was much closer to $8,000 per girl.

Both purses and the number of rodeos are going up, Lydia says. There are more than 600 rodeos that girls can participate in, and the total purse money is now well over $500,000, Lydia reports.

When girls first started competing in rodeo, back in 1948, they rode for nothing. And in 1958, they were still riding for practically nothing. That year, the guaranteed purse for the whole season was only $29,000.

But things have changed, including the types of rodeo events open to the girls.

At first, it was just barrel racing. Now the girls compete in breakaway calf roping, tie down calf roping, goat tying, bull riding, team roping, steer undecorating and bareback bronc riding.

While the girls like competing in a sport normally considered to be a man's sport, their participation in tough events has nothing to do with today's ballyhoo about women's lib, says Lydia.

"GRA recognizes the strong point of its appeal is the element of glamour the girls add to the overall rodeo program."

GRA even requires its contestants to ride in every grand entry and wear colorful western clothes at all times.

Just as rodeo cowboys, the girls are independent athletes, totally responsible for all their expenses, travel and equipment. They pay their entry fees, ride in their event, and hope to make a profit. And just as it is for the men, nothing is guaranteed.

Cut It Out!

There is always a special place in my heart for the horse which earns his keep.

I could really like Mr. San Peppy, the 1976 World Champion cutting horse, who earned a record $34,065.61 last year. It's a pretty safe guess the King Ranch of Kingsville, Texas, is fairly fond of him, too.

The 8-year-old stallion was ridden to the world championship by Buster Welch of Merkel, Texas, now the only rider in history to win four such championships. He won twice on a horse named Marion's Girl and twice on Mr. San Peppy.

But what really twanged the purse strings of my heart was $11,022.53 won by 15-year-old Larry Shearin of Creve Coeur, Mo. He won the loot on his 18-year-old gelding Royal Hank.

I suddenly realized my daughter Cathy might happily be pushed into the ranks of the employed without violating a single child labor law.

Excitedly, I called Dr. Wesley P. Helzer of Chino, Calif. Dr. Helzer is a chiropractor who practices most often on humans, occasionally on horses, and is frequently called upon to "straighten up" a less than perfect cutting horse. Doc Helzer, as he is known to horsemen, has been a cutting horse man for many years. He once had a cutting horse school and now he spends his free time studying and filming cutting horses.

He quickly shattered my dream of sudden wealth through the enforced labor of my daughter by saying, "Don, it takes time, lots of work, plenty of patience, plus an exceptionally fine horse."

The birthplace of cutting horses was the open range, where the horse was said to have been born of necessity.

"No system better than the cutting horse has been devised to separate a single animal from a herd of cattle and prevent its return with a minimum of disturbance," Helzer said.

The first recorded cutting competition for prize money was held at the Cowboy Reunion in Haskell, Texas, in 1898. Early cutting contests were an immediate success, grew in popularity, and in 1946, were placed under a uniform set of rules when the National Cutting Horse Association was formed.

A cutting contest begins, Doc Helzer says, when 15 to 20 head of cattle are held at one end of an arena by two riders called herd holders.

"When the name of the contesting horse is called, the horse is moved into the herd to begin work. One cow is separated from the herd and driven past the herd holders toward the center of the arena where two more riders are stationed to turn the cow back toward the imagined safety of the herd," Helzer explains.

As the calf or yearling dodges and twists to get by the cutting horse, the horse makes counter moves to hold the critter where he is.

For two and a half minutes, the horse must roll swiftly to the left or right, stop, change direction, move forward, fall back, and always stay head to head with the cow being worked.

The rider may not help the horse. As a matter of fact, Doc Helzer says, the reactions of a good horse are actually too fast for the rider. A good rider on a great horse simply tries to be as little hinderance to the horse as possible.

After getting the desired challenge from one cow, the horse may be signaled to stop by his rider and may be returned to the herd to begin another demonstration of his cutting ability.

While the cutting horse performs, one or more judges evaluate how hard he is challenged by the stock, how he handles himself in meeting the challenges, and what mistakes, if any, he makes.

The judge gives each horse a score of between 60 and 80 points. The highest score wins the contest.

Always exciting, cutting contests now are attracting a lot more riders who are going after the prize money. The National Cutting Horse Association (NCHA) approves more than 750 open and championship cuttings each year, and NCHA receives results from more than 400 shows which have cutting contests for novice horses.

Keeping in mind the prize money and a few suggestions from Doc Helzer, Cathy begins cutting practice at 6 a.m. tomorrow. Is that too early?

Insurance Can Be Tricky

The exclusion will get you if you don't watch out! Insurance isn't one of the favorite topics of conversation among horsemen. Technicalities don't count for much.

Among horsemen, you either roped the steer or you didn't. You won the class or you didn't. You rode the bronc or you didn't. Horsemen don't dwell on technicalities and they don't look for, nor readily accept, excuses.

The only grays in the life of a horseman are dapple grays.

And because horsemen are horsemen, they rarely think about insurance claims, exclusions, comparative negligence, or care, custody or control of the property of others.

But they'd better!

I ran a little survey during one of my college horsemanship courses and found:

Eighty-eight percent of the students had homeowner's insurance, which they expected would cover them against personal injury liability or property damage liability.

However, 30 percent had engaged in a single pursuit which might negate their coverage. Seventy-three percent had engaged in another activity which might negate their coverage.

Another 38 per cent had claimed a tax deduction for horse-related expenses, but did not carry business insurance. And 46 percent had taken care of a friend's horse at one time or another, which could result in "no coverage under specific circumstances."

They were all potential victims of the insurance exclusion or "technicality."

Bill Roberts, an attorney who defends against all types of personal injury claims, and Vic Tyler, an insurance agent, agree insurance and horses can be tricky business.

The ownership of horses often involves business ventures — whether intentionally planned or not — which are excluded under the comprehensive personal liability coverage of a homeowner's policy, they said.

For example, if the horse owner has a mare and the mare has a foal, and the foal is sold, the insurance carrier could disclaim coverage, saying the sale of the foal constituted a business venture.

If a family buys a horse, then sells it, is that a business?

Debatable!

If the family already owns several horses for personal use, does the family need another one? Or was the horse purchased with the idea of reselling it and making money? If the idea was to make money, the insurance carrier may say the homeowner's coverage no longer applies to any activity involving horses.

With very minor exceptions, every personal liability policy excludes the property of others while in your care, Tyler says.

The concept of comparative negligence, now the rule in nearly half the states, holds the horseman responsible for making a judgment about information provided by another.

If a friend says he can ride, but falls off and is hurt, the horseman may be held liable. If the horseman misjudged the friend's ability by 40 percent, he may be held 40 percent liable for the accident.

As silly as it seems, you may be responsible for the dude who tells you a lie, or the equipment he failed to fix properly, or the hole in the trail he may fall into. The courts may say you should have warned him about the hole, and if you did warn him, the court might say your warning wasn't strong enough.

Scary? You bet!

What kind of insurance should you have?

See an agent, and ask about a homeowner's policy with an endorsement to include incidental business pursuits, or a "farmers" comprehensive personal liability or comprehensive general liability policy, Tyler advises.

Under some circumstances, you can extend your personal liability policy, or you may want a $1-million umbrella policy. In any case, check it out and decide which is best for you.

You'll probably never be sued by a real horseman. Real horsemen understand and assume the risks involved in being around horses. Only dudes want someone else to pay for their mistakes.

But until all the dudes become horsemen, the exclusion will get you, if you don't watch out!

Taxing Your Nerves

Horses and taxes are hard to figure.

If you have horses for recreation and pleasure, any expenses connected with them are not deductible.

However, as any helpful IRS investigator will tell you, if receipts from your recreation and pleasure should somehow exceed the expenses – the profit is taxable as income.

The rule of the taxable horse: Income is income, but outgo gets ignored.

If you use Form 1040, the only deductions allowed a horse owner are the ones allowed every individual. Namely, taxes, interest, capital and casualty losses. Thus, if the county tax assessor has already taxed your backyard horse, you are allowed to deduct that additional tax. If you borrowed money to buy the horse, or a trailer, or a barn, you may deduct the interest.

If you bought a horse, then sold it at a loss, deduct the loss on Schedule D. However, if you sold the horse at a profit, you've got to show it on Schedule D.

Other than that, you're out a buck or two.

Unless you establish your horse operation as a business.

In which case, the profit motive must be present and some type of economic activity must be involved. And the taxpayer must devote a substantial amount of his time to the business.

Two characteristic elements of a business are regularity of activity, and the production of profit. But unfortunately, profit isn't a necessary byproduct of business.

In a horse-related business, you need to show a profit in two out of seven consecutive years. Unless that general rule is disallowed, which can happen.

If you have a horse business, you can deduct all ordinary and necessary expenses incurred in carrying out that business.

You are disallowed any personal living or family expenses, such as a new pair of socks for your boots. They may be necessary to warm feet, but not to the selling of a horse for profit.

New chaps or silver on a headstall could be considered both ordinary and necessary since it is nearly impossible to win at a horse show without them. And not winning can easily cost a business its expected profit.

Car expenses are sometimes hard to justify, but it can easily be argued that a truck, with trailer hitch and ranch name displayed on the side, is a legitimate business expense.

If your home is also your business location, then a percentage of household expenses can be allocated to the business. For example, if you use one room of a 10-room house as an office, then 10 per cent of the light, heat, rent, telephone, etc., is a business expense.

If you purchase a horse for $1,000, you can recover this capital expenditure by claiming depreciation over the life expectancy of the horse.

All of the above suggestions for deductions may

result in a careful perusal of your return by the Internal Revenue Service.

First, keep accurate records of all expenses and income and be sure each is documented by a receipt, bill or invoice.

Second, call the nearest IRS office for an opinion if you have the slightest doubt about your return.

And finally, if you make a profit, you may be subject to payment of self-employment social security taxes and estimated income taxes.

And remember, Thursday is visiting day at Leavenworth.

CHAPTER VIII

One Man's Opinion

If the horse industry continues to move in its present direction and at its present pace, it may be self-destructive.

Much of what we preach and practice as being good is really bad. And much of what we don't talk about or ignore is far more important than the things we label as important.

A recent survey by the American Association of Equine Practitioners to determine the most prevalent types of lameness and their causes should be a red flag to all horsemen.

Survey results lead us to the conclusion that certain strains of horses produce a larger percentage of unsound horses than others.

And those strains are the heavy-bodied, light-boned horses.

What do we look for today in the show ring? Horses with heavy bodies and refined bones. Those are our halter champions.

Another conclusion: Subjecting young horses, especially two-year-olds, to work stress definitely contributes to unsoundness.

And what are we doing? We're offering more and larger purses at the racetracks for the younger runners, the 2- and 3-year-olds. And we are pushing show horses to perform more complicated exercises, with greater stress, at an earlier age. We think it is good if a junior horse (one under the age of 4) can be a halter champion, a pleasure champion and a reining champion all at the same time.

The survey concluded also that horses are more prone to go lame for some trainers than for others.

Obviously, the pressure to get horses ready sooner and win at an early age causes trainers to push horses beyond reasonable expectations, and today, the most successful trainer is measured by how many times he wins. No record is kept of how many horses he has broken down.

There is no award for the trainer who gets the most from a horse while keeping the horse sound. In fact, many show and race standards have been lowered so sore horses can be given drugs to eliminate the pain while they work.

The survey revealed laminitis and other hoof conditions were the most common causes of lameness in the fore limb. These were closely followed by navicular disease, fractured sesamoids, carpitis and sprains. Next in order were bowed tendons, ring bones, suspensory ligament involvements and carpal chips, followed by fracture of the splint bones, side bones, buck shins, and splints.

All of the above are leg and hoof problems normally caused by one or two things, or by a combination of both. The two are: rapid growth and heavy bodies putting too much weight on the young, soft bone, or too much stress too early, well before a horse is in condition to withstand stress.

The more than 200 veterinarians participating in the survey reported the following, in order of importance, as the largest contributors to unsoundess: 1. conformation; 2. nutrition; 3. too early use; 4. heredity.

I think we are attempting to improve the conformation of our horses, but we are still allowing the indiscriminate breeding of poorly-conformed animals.

Breed associations must soon take the unpopular position of only registering the get of qualified stallions and mares, and of emphasizing the standard of conformation as it relates to soundness.

We are smart to understand the importance of good nutrition. Are we too dumb to put a stop to the use of rapid growth supplements, hormone shots and other gimmick foods which are contributing to the breakdown of young animals?

There must be a new emphasis placed on the work of older horses. Racetracks should establish races and big purses for older horses which have been kept sound. And special awards should be presented to the trainers of performance horses which show year after year without lameness.

Horses which show signs of lameness must, not 'should,' be excused from the ring. There is no reason to work a lame horse.

Finally, we must do more to eliminate the breeding of horses which have a predisposition to lameness.

All of these points will be argued, ignored, put off and shuffled aside. Virtually no one wants to rock the boat of financial reward, or change what appears to be a favorable status quo.

But I maintain good changes can be made without financial loss. It's a matter of information, communications and reestablishment of priorities.

Licensing Is Needed

Licensing of show and pleasure horse trainers is long overdue.

So is the licensing of riding instructors.

It would force an increase in education. It would eliminate a lot of cruelty to animals. It would require the upgrading of riding skills.

It also would put many people out of work.

How would the "beat 'em and knock 'em around" novices make a buck? How would the "ride like a sack of potatoes" lady next door support her horse habit?

Why, we might end up just like most of the European countries, where horsemanship is a highly regarded skill, an art form which requires education, knowledge and years of study and practice.

Licensing of riding instructors, for example, might result in a formation of an organization such as the British Horse Society (BHS), whose certificate holders are respected worldwide for having reached a high standard of equestrian skills.

And can you imagine? Some young American radicals are going to Britain to study for the BHS examinations.

Before being accepted, they must be able to ride at all gaits, jump a horse and have a basic knowledge of horse care. Once accepted, they become either working pupils or students.

A working pupil pays $15 to $25 a week for accommodations, instructions and the opportunity to work from 6:30 a.m. to 7 p.m. cleaning stalls, grooming horses, caring for tack, exercising and feeding horses, listening to lecturers, taking riding instruction and learning teaching techniques. In their spare time, they must read the theory of riding and training.

A working pupil spends a minimum of six months to a year in training.

A student pays $50 to $125 a week and gets a more concentrated course of study usually completed in three or four months.

A student receives two to three hours per day of

riding and teaching instruction, plus lectures on all other aspects of horse care.

A student practices stall and tack cleaning, horse exercising and feeding, etc., but does not have to work quite as hard as the working pupil. The student's day ends at 6 p.m. except when he or she is scheduled for late duty.

When the study course is completed, the students take a four-part, one-day examination at a BHS center.

Candidates for the certificate take a riding test first. They must demonstrate a good seat, ability to apply the proper aids, a knowledge of basic gaits, and they must complete standard school movements. They must also be able to jump a horse from the trot and the canter over fences of three feet, three inches. The course includes double fences and changes of direction.

The second part of the examination is about stable management and includes a demonstration of daily stable routine, the care of stabled horses and horses at grass. This section includes an oral exam on feeding, watering, grooming, bandaging, exercising, recognition of lameness or ill health, preparing and caring for horses during a journey, care of competition horses, clipping, plaiting and trimming. The student also must demonstrate a complete knowledge of conformation, saddlery and shoeing.

The third section deals with minor ailments and includes a 45-minute written examination covering the treatment for all manner of wounds, fractures, etc.

The final part of the examination requires the candidate to give a riding lesson to four to six persons.

The candidate must show he has a sound knowledge of basic equitation, can apply basic principles of teaching, can improve the ability of the students, knows the principles of safety and can proceed in case of an accident or emergency.

I tell you, if these young radicals keep learning and

studying and improving their equestrian skills, one of these days they'll start changing the status quo.

And then where will the horse business be?

Cruel Trainers Need A Lesson

Everyone who knows me is quite aware I'm a gentle soul not subject to fits of temper. I'm an open-minded man, tolerant, with only a minor number of prejudices.

Simply reading some of my thoughts about the stupid, idiotic, bungling efforts of some dippy dude will demonstrate my temperate attitude. I might even cloak my disgust for a dangerously ridiculous device for horses such as the Running W, and I'd be very careful never to openly criticize another trainer's techniques. And the only thing I would say about a man or woman who advocates the use of a Running W is that he or she is a . . .

Maybe an example will make the point.

The Running W is a long rope or leather strap which is attached by one end to the horse's left front ankle with a hobble. It is run up the left front leg to an "O" ring on the cinch, run back to the right front ankle, attached there to a hobble, then run up the right foreleg to another "O" ring on the cinch, and then out to the hands of the trainer. The line forms a W shape.

The idea is to pull hard enough on the end of the line to drop the horse to his front knees, often causing him to slam his head into the ground or go over on his side. This treatment is supposed to discourage the "killer" from attempting to kill you.

Ordinarily this training procedure begins without a rider. And that seems to be the only sensible thing about the whole matter.

The horse is then deliberately spooked, startled or driven to rage by the trainer, who then drops the horse savagely to prove to the horse his misbehavior doesn't pay.

Once the horse is sufficiently bruised and broken, and a rider without a great deal of mental capacity is located, the horse is mounted.

Again, the trainer deliberately incites the horse to misbehave, and again, drops him by yanking the horse's front legs from under him. This frequently causes both horse and rider to be half buried in the dirt.

Advocates of this method believe if you brutalize the horse long enough and use this device, you will cure the horse of his problems, which most often is not liking to be spooked, spurred or whipped.

I believe that what you get as the end result is two dummies and a victim. The dummies are half disappointed they can't go on proving their superiority, and the victim is now well-schooled in hate and anger.

Rather than fly into a rage about the Running W, I'd prefer to quietly and gently attach it to the trainer. I'd be open-minded enough to listen to his pleas for mercy. And then, of course, I'd incite him to misbehavior and drop him.

I admire the person without prejudice who is tolerant of the ideas of others.

It's things like the Running W and people stupid enough to use them I can't stand.

Horses Are Too Fat

The horse show ring today is "fat city."

Our performance horses are too fat!

Most winning halter horses are much too fat.

A popular saying among horsemen, "The best color is fat," helps load on the weight.

And the prepared-feed manufacturers are doing their best to turn horses into porkers. Practically every heavy food processor has at least one growth and weight producing supplement on the market.

In fact, the rush to fat is so intense these days

many breeders and trainers are shooting young horses full of hormones to stimulate growth and gain additional unneeded weight.

Why?

Simply to win. Fat horses win. Skinny horses don't. So, fat is the fad, right or wrong.

And what's the result?

The ability of our performance horses to do hard work is decreasing. Most of them are simply too fat to perform standard exercises with grace. They are so overweight, in some cases, they can't lift their forehand or drive properly with their hindquarters.

Many halter horses are so overweight they often break down before they get a chance to become performance horses. (Check the record and see how few of the top halter horses ever become winning performance horses.)

Overweight horses never become supple enough to work well. They lose their lateral flexibility, their wind and their endurance.

While learning the standard of performance in older horses, this infatuation with super growth is raising something else — the number of incidences of epiphysitis in young horses.

Epiphysitis is a condition in which the growth plates of the legs are literally crushed by excess weight. Now a fairly common problem, epiphysitis shows up most often in the knees and ankles of horses under the age of three.

On each end of the shaft of the long bone — forearm and cannon — is the epiphysis, or cartilage, which has not yet turned to bone. It is here the growth and length takes place.

Epiphysitis is an inflammation of the epiphyseal plate, according to Dr. Richard J. Brown, DVM. He says the condition can occur on any long bone, but commonly relates to the knee and ankle.

Many horsemen refer to epiphysitis of the ankle

as "big ankles," "double knees" or "hour-glass ankles."

When epiphysitis occurs, the epiphyseal plate is damaged by pressure, resulting in inflammatory swelling, which gives a knobby and rough appearance to the joint. Usually there is a distinctive hour-glass shape. Unless severe, says Dr. Brown, lameness is not always associated with epiphysitis, but appears later with the resulting breakdown of other physical structures.

Dr. Brown believes excessive weight has a relationship to epiphysitis, but also stresses rapid growth rate, and large muscle masses in proportion to bone structure are major contributory causes.

Dr. Brown says that in diagnosed cases of epiphysitis, he often recommends slowing the colt's growth rate, taking him off supplements and controlling nutrition.

Don't get caught in the fat fad.

You don't want a skinny, underfed, or diseased horse. Neither do I.

But big (fat), isn't any better.

While many show horses are too fat, the high cost of feed, plus ignorance on the part of the owner, are causing just the opposite problem for a lot of backyard horses.

Capt. Bill Virden of the San Diego Humane Society reported 738 underfed horses were impounded in San Diego County in 1975.

"You would be amazed at how many horse lovers don't know what bare ribs look like," he said.

"We actually had to go out and tell horse owners how to feed their animals."

String 'Em Up!

Hang 'em high.

That would be my penalty for horse thieves.

And I don't think it's cruel or unusual punishment.

Foes of capital punishment will claim the threat of hanging won't deter criminals, but I say it's hard for a dead horse thief to steal another horse.

A hundred years ago, there were more horses and less horse thieves. Hanging was the penalty for stealing a horse in many states. Today, both the number of horses and the number of horse thefts are on the increase. The penalties vary from state to state, but all are relatively mild.

A rustler in Texas recently stole a $150,000 Thoroughbred and sold her to a slaughterhouse for 22 cents a pound. He was caught, convicted and fined $2,000.

A rustler in Southern California presently is buying horses with bad checks, then driving nails in their feet to make them lame so he can sell them for dog food at about 30 cents a pound.

But the dollar value loss is nothing compared to the emotional pain suffered by owners of stolen horses.

A friend had a 7-year-old mare which she had been training since the horse was two. They had been friends for five years, learning together, competing together, meeting the day-to-day challenges together. When the mare was sick or injured, it was the woman who cared for her. When the woman wanted a quiet friend to listen and share her burdens, she confided in the mare as they rode across the rolling hills.

Rustlers used bolt cutters to snap the chain which locked the mare's corral. The mare is gone. Where? Who knows? Hopefully, out of state where she might have been sold to someone who would take care of her. But most likely she was lamed, then taken to a slaughterhouse and sold for a few dollars.

Revenge and punishment of those who stole her won't replace the mare. Nothing will replace her. She was an individual who had her own way of saying hello or of trying to please.

No, revenge is not the answer.

But removal of the person committing such a crime is not unthinkable. I can see no redeeming value for mankind in such a person.

A convicted horse thief walks the horse auction yards of Southern California weekly. I know he stole several horses. I know he has bought horses with bad checks. I know he will steal again. And yet our system of justice allows him to try again. If he gets caught and if he gets convicted, and if he doesn't get off on some technicality, he will be punished by being placed on probation again.

The California Penal Code lists the stealing of horses as grand theft, which carries a penalty of not more than one year in a county jail or not more than 10 years in a state prison.

While the conviction rate is called 'pretty good' by law enforcement agencies, most agree there is a tendency on the part of judges to reduce sentences. That translates to little or no time in jail and/or a light fine.

What can an individual horse owner do while horsemen work collectively at getting the law and the penalties changed? As with most things, the honest guy has to get meaner and take more precautions.

According to Sgt. Bill Bacon of the Los Angeles County Sheriff's Office, preventive action by horse owners is the only recourse now. Sergeant Bacon is one of two officers assigned full time to the horse theft problem in Los Angeles County.

"There's less tendency to steal a horse which carries a brand," Sergeant Bacon says. "But most owners don't want to brand their horses, thinking it is painful to the animal or believing it disfigures them.

It's also a good idea to file an identification form with your local sheriff's office. The form should identify the horse adequately and a picture of the horse should be attached.

Horse owners are "too friendly," Sergeant Bacon believes.

"They let people come on their property and look around. They'll even take strangers on a tour to show them their best horses and in the process, the best way to steal them.

"Be suspicious," Sergeant Brown advises. "Ask questions and find out who is looking over your place. If you see a strange car or truck, get the license number and report it to the police.

"Don't wait until the horse is gone and then think about the strangers who were wandering around the place."

Night lights deter thefts, as do big dogs and good locks and chains on corrals. Keep all fences in good repair, he suggests.

Be especially suspicious of young girls, Sergeant Bacon cautions. A lot of horse thieves today are girls, some as young as 15 years old.

Although figures are obscure, it would appear that horse thefts have more than doubled nationally. And it looks as if it is going to get worse before it gets better.

While most law enforcement agencies lump horse thefts with all animal thefts and therefore don't have specific data available, almost all of them agree the numbers are getting larger, and sadly, that only half of the horses which have been stolen are ever recovered.

Don't Fool Mother Nature

Happy birthday to you, happy birthday to you . . .

Who's happy about Jan. 1 being the official birthday for more registered horses?

Certainly not the new foal.

Not the mare. Not the stallion. Not the owners, nor the exhibitors.

Then who?

The bookkeepers, that's who!

To make it convenient for record keepers, Jan. 1

was established as the official birthday for horses by most breed registries, regardless of what month the horse was foaled. And that means a young horse, whether 6 days, 6 weeks, or 6 months old, becomes 1 year old on the Jan. 1 following his birth, and thereafter leaps into a new age bracket with the passing of each calendar year.

Foals and mares don't like the Jan. 1 birthday. It's a cold, wet, windy, snowy, silly time to be born.

It's not nice to fool Mother Nature, who knows it's best for horses to be born in the late spring, when the temperatures are warmer and the grass is greener.

Mother Nature shows her displeasure at man's attempts to force artificial early breeding seasons by giving the horse a low conception rate (the average being less than 50 percent) and a high fatality rate among newborns. The conception rate exceeds 70 percent only at the very best breeding establishments.

According to studies by Dr. O. J. Ginther at the University of Wisconsin, the best time for breeding mares is May 12 to Oct. 10, which means the foal would appear approximately 11 months, 10 days later, or anywhere from April to September.

And studies done by Colorado State University have established the best breeding time for stallions is in June. Semen output is highest during the latter part of the established breeding season, double in July what it is in January.

But with Jan. 1 being the official birthday, show and race horse owners refuse to think of waiting to breed mares in July and August. They believe it is to their advantage to have a foal born as close to Jan. 1 as possible because an early foal should be bigger, stronger, better-muscled and faster than one born later in the year, even though they are, on the record book, the same age.

And show judges seem to think the same way. They usually pick the largest, most mature-looking horses in a class. (It's the subject of much conversation when a judge picks a young horse over older stallions or mares in a grand champion class.)

But Mother Nature may be fooling us all.

The records show that even though we are attempting to force an early birthday so we'll have more winners, it isn't working.

A study by the American Quarter Horse Association of winners of the world's richest race, the All American Futurity, during a 10-year period reveals one winner was foaled in January, two in February, three in March, one in April, two in May, and one in June. The average birth date was March 27.

Two more random studies showed the average birth date of 73 AQHA champions to be March 28. And the average birth date of 829 Registry of Merit winners was April 8.

Anyway, happy birthday to all horses on their official birthday, Jan. 1, even though the date is costing horses and horsemen dearly in wasted time, trouble and dollars.

March 1 would be a better official birthday. Let the bookkeepers enter that in their records.

If You Go, Go To Win

If you go into the show ring, then go to win!

Believe you're a winner. Ride like a winner. Have the confidence of a winner. Give every show and every class your best effort.

Here are 10 tips which will help you win.

1. Know the name of the judge.

I keep a little record book of judges to remind me of what a particular judge likes and what he or she dislikes. Some judges prefer the type of horses I ride. Some do not. If the judge likes my horses, I make an effort to be at the show. If I've not done well before a particular judge, I stay home.

If a judge likes a horse to bridle, then drive your horse onto the bit and keep his head tucked. If you know the judge likes a loose rein, ride on a loose rein.

2. Arrive at the show early and be prepared.

The last thing you and your horse need is a lot of rushing around to make a class on time. By getting to the show early, you'll have time to prepare your horse and yourself in every detail. By class time, you'll both be relaxed and well-groomed, and that's important if you want to be a winner.

Most judges, including myself, are impressed by the horse and rider which presents a perfect picture. For some reason, shining horses and smartly-dressed riders just seem to work better.

3. Start showing the minute you enter the show ring.

Judging isn't easy, so any help you can give the judge is appreciated. Start things off right by demonstrating to the judge you have entered the class to win, and give him a reason to like you immediately. The minute your horse's nose is inside the ring, do everything possible to win the class.

4. Watch the judge. Be polite and listen to him.

If you are in a pleasure or equitation class, keep an eye on the judge at all times. You can pay close attention without being obvious.

If you are in a class which calls for individual work, be very polite and listen carefully. So many young riders tend to jump into an exercise without having been asked to do so. Or, believe it or not, they want to argue with the judge about his instructions.

5. Stay in a good position on the rail.

If the class is large, it's hard for the judge to see everyone. Get in a good position and maintain it. Don't crowd other horses or get blocked by other horses. If you have to circle to find an open spot, do it. The judge will appreciate your efforts, providing your moves are not obvious attempts to catch his eye. Always work the rail, moving away only to pass a slower-working horse or go around a horse which is misbehaving.

6. Work slowly and smoothly.

When asked to change gaits, don't be the first to react to the instructions, be the smartest. A good judge will give you more credit if your transitions are smooth, so take your time.

7. Smile and show confidence.

Again, judges are human, and being human, are impressed by the rider who seems confident and relaxed. If you've been to a few shows, then you've heard trainers and parents tell young riders to, "Smile. Look happy." It's good advice which winners have been passing on to winners for years.

8. Know what is happening ahead of you.

Many riders are so intent on what they're doing, they fail to look ahead and anticipate problem areas or notice the troubles of other riders. Smart riders keep an eye out for potential trouble ahead and take corrective action before they end up in the middle of it.

9. Recover quickly from mistakes.

Good show riders make mistakes, too, but judges have a tendency to overlook mistakes if they're not too obvious. Don't make a big deal out of a mistake. Correct the mistake calmly and quickly, but not in such a hurry that you compound the error. Then get on with the business of showing to win.

10. Don't help your competition.

You paid your entry fee and you have as much right as anyone to ride in the class. Be a good sport. Don't cause problems, but don't go out of your way to help someone else win.

Yes, I'm all for good sportsmanship, and showing should be fun, I agree. And it is, when you're winning!

Wild On The Range

The wild horse problem can be solved, but . . .

It won't be solved by emotional sentimentality.

It won't be solved by the Bureau of Land Management's Adopt a Horse program.

And it won't be solved by groups such as The American Horse Protection Association, which I suspect spends more on administration and slick material than on the welfare of the wild horse.

I believe we should save the wild horse in America, but the methods being used now won't do it.

In 1971, we had a wild horse population of about 17,000. Today, there are more than 60,000 wild horses. At the rate they are multiplying – between 18 and 25 percent each year – we'll have 72,000 in 1978; 90,000 in 1979, and 108,000 in 1980. If that progression continues, what we'll have in a few years is 20,000 to 30,000 wild horses starving to death each year.

By an act of Congress, the Bureau of Land Management has been given three options to save the wild horses. It can capture them and have them adopted. It can relocate them to natural habitats, or it can destroy some of them.

The Adopt-A-Horse program went into effect in May of 1976, and has placed about 1,500 horses, according to Nancy Manzi of the bureau's Washington, D.C., office.

The program has three major flaws.

1. It's impossible to adopt a wild horse. A wild horse is wild. Confined, he can't run free across the range with his mane and tail flying in the wind, symbolizing his romantic past and the American dream. He'll be a miserable, captive mustang, and more than likely, he'll hurt someone.

2. There are not enough people to adopt wild horses, and there is no way to make sure the horses are well cared for once they are adopted.

3. The wild horses are multiplying at a rate of 12,000 a year, while the adoption rate is about 2,000 a year.

Relocation to other public lands is not a viable answer since most of the land is already saturated with horses or already overgrazed. We have only enough public lands to supply 20,000 wild horses adequately.

Finally, the Bureau of Land Management won't brave the public outcry which would surely follow the destruction of some of the horses.

So what is to be done and who will do it?

There are already hundreds of well-established organizations which can demand, and get, a wild horse protection act which establishes a minimum size herd and a guarantee of adequate grazing range. The law needs teeth and a severe penalty for violators.

There needs to be a comprehensive educational program attached to the protection act so the public is aware of what is being done.

The public must also stop believing the inaccurate, tear-jerking stories of saving "the last wild horse," and demand that any fund-seeking organization tell in detail its program, its expenditures, its accomplishments and its failures.

Finally, we need a good herd management program which could be administered by a college or university, a horsemen's organization, or a state or federal agency which would answer to a private organization.

And if you are wondering if a good herd management program would mean destroying weak, older or diseased animals, the answer is YES.

It is nature's law that some things die so that others may live. Mankind has refused to live with nature.

If we want our wild horses and everything else, too, then we must at least compromise with nature.

If we can't accept that, then all the wild horses will eventually die of starvation, overcrowding, a reversal of public opinion, or capture and imprisonment.

I want to know that at least some of them will run free forever.

Road To Oblivion

I know I sound like an old fuddy-duddy.

And when I get on my soapbox, the response will be, "Impossible. There's no place else to ride. I have no trailer." Or, "It's the only way to get to my friend's house, etc."

I don't care. Get those horses off the highway!

Highways, cars and horses don't mix. They never will. And it doesn't matter how careful you are. There will be accidents. They can be serious, even fatal.

There's no such thing as a minor accident with a child, a horse, pavement and/or a car. And if the rider and horse only suffer abrasions, that's a miracle, not an accident.

And don't tell me, "Accidents just happen. You're over reacting." Because I'll reply, "One paralyzed child or one death is one too many when the accident could have been avoided.

Unfortunately, people will go on riding their horses on the highways in spite of my protests. They'll argue the population is growing and the open land is shrinking, that we are not developing riding areas as fast as we are producing new riders, and that the trail systems everywhere are inadequate.

I agree, but I'm still against highway riding.

But if you still insist on riding your horse along the highway, at least keep these points in mind.

You should school a green horse in light traffic areas as much as you can before you go out for that first, and possibly last, pleasure ride.

The horse needs to become as familiar as possible with cars, motorcycles, farm machinery, dogs, bicycles, litter and blowing paper. And remember, it is most often the sight of unfamiliar objects rather than sound which frightens horses.

Look then for the things which will frighten the horse, and prepare yourself and your horse. You cannot relax your vigil for a moment. You must pick out the "shies and spookies" first.

Your horse must be shod if you are going to ride on pavement. I'd recommend you have your farrier put on shoes with a calk to grip the pavement. Horses slip easily on pavement, especially cement.

If you do a lot of pavement riding, then leather pads and shoes will help keep your horse sound for a few months longer. The leather reduces the concussion the horse suffers from hard surface riding.

It's a good idea to ride with friends, especially if you are riding a green horse. Always ride single file. If you ride side by side, you make a larger target for vehicular traffic.

It also reduces the amount of control you have over the horse and limits the direction in which you can move quickly, should it be necessary. But don't separate and ride on both sides of the road. It's more dangerous if traffic has to weave in and out of horses.

When you are crossing the pavement, move your horse out at a walk. Don't turn your horse on the pavement and don't change gaits.

If you have started across a highway and a car suddenly appears, don't stop and turn back.

Move your horse on across the road without exciting him. Better still, when you cross well-traveled roads, dismount and walk your horse across.

Riding at night is even more dangerous, especially riding at dusk. But if you insist on this practice, wrap reflective safety strips around your horse's cannon bones. You should also wrap his tail with a white tail wrap.

You should wear white or light-colored clothing. Carry a flashlight so you can shine it ahead and avoid rocks and holes.

Remember, most drivers don't own horses and don't understand them, so the safety of you and your horse . . . and possibly the driver . . . is up to you.

Riding along the highway is a bad practice, and I'm

completely opposed to it. But if you continue, knowing the danger, do it as sensibly and cautiously as possible.

Where From Here?

Just off to the north, not too far from the barn, there is a gradual grassy slope which runs up to the mountains.

It takes about an hour to ride to the point where the sage and rocks rise up from the rolling grazing land. In the springtime, the California poppies wave a golden greeting as the horse jogs through their territory. But in winter, the grass is brown and the wind blows cold and the sky is winter clear.

There is time and quiet on the ride, and a chance to reflect on what has gone before and what is coming.

The horse population is growing at its most rapid rate in history.

I can't help wonder, however, where all the horses will go or who will ride this hill when it's covered with homes and roads and swimming pools and fences, as 'progress' dictates it soon will be.

I have no doubt the problems created by more houses and more people and more cars and more buildings and less open area and less farm land and less water will be conquered. The rules and regulations involved in the solutions will be established by the government, making some people happy and others not so happy.

The wars are coming.

Throughout history, the horse never hesitated to carry his master into battle. But who will now do battle for the horse?

There are a lot of national, state, regional and local organizations supposedly looking after the horse and the interests of horsemen.

But in terms of real issues, there isn't one worth its fancy stationery.

Such organizations are conciliatory, slow, self-centered and afraid to attack. They react. They don't initiate. They've closed the barn door after the horse is out.

A single organization representing all breeds and all horsemen must be formed immediately. It must be a strong and aggressive organization which will accept the challenge of planning and then making sure things happen which will benefit the horse.

If horsemen don't do it, it will be done to them.

Once interest in any subject grows, as it has with horses, the foremost need of those who become intrigued is the need for information.

An attempt is being made by some private organizations, some colleges and some individuals to provide information about horses and their care and handling. But it is not enough.

Injuries to horses and riders are increasing at astounding rates. Horses are not being fed properly, housed, cared for, bred, exercised, ridden, trained, or treated for diseases. Not because horsemen don't care or aren't willing, but simply because they are ignorant, and the information that would help them isn't readily available from qualified sources.

But even those of us who like to believe we are well-informed aren't doing enough. We haven't yet demanded that riding instructors know anything about riding, or that trainers understand even the simplest principles of horse psychology. Our system of selecting horse show judges is a laughing matter.

Horsemen have accepted all the good from the horse — the pleasure of his company, the toil of his muscle and bone, the quiet patience, the willing effort, the silent acceptance of punishment. They take joy in his accomplishments and admire his natural grace, vitality and beauty.

But horsemen haven't yet faced up to the reality of today. It's complex and difficult, but we must soon